ARTHUR MILLER

The Last Yankee

with commentary and notes by
KATHERINE EGERTON

Series Editor: Enoch Brater

METHUEN DRAMA

Methuen Drama Student Edition

10 9 8 7 6 5 4 3 2 1

This edition first published in the United Kingdom in 2011 by
Methuen Drama
A & C Black Publishers Limited
36 Soho Square
London W1D 3QY
www.methuendrama.com

Chronology of Arthur Miller by Enoch Brater, with grateful thanks to the Arthur Miller
Society for permission to draw on their 'Brief Chronology of Arthur Miller's Life and
Works'

A CIP catalogue record for this book is available from the British Library

ISBN 978 1 408 12315 7

Commentary and notes typeset by SX Composing DTP, Rayleigh, Essex
Playtext typeset by Country Setting, Kingsdown, Kent
Printed and bound in Great Britain by
CPI Cox & Wyman Ltd, Reading, Berkshire

Contents

I would like to thank my assistant, Brittney Morris, for her contribution to this volume.

K.E.

Arthur Miller: 1915–2005

1915   17 October: Arthur Asher Miller born in New York City, the second of Isidore (Izzy) and Augusta (Gussie) Barnett Miller's three children. His brother Kermit born in 1912, sister Joan 1922.

1920–28   Attends PS 24 in Harlem, then an upper-middle-class Jewish neighbourhood, where his mother went to the same school. The family lives in an apartment overlooking Central Park on the top floor of a six-storey building at 45 West 110th Street, between Lenox and Fifth Avenues. Takes piano lessons, goes to Hebrew school and ice-skates in the park. His Barnett grandparents are nearby on West 118th Street. In summers the extended family rents a bungalow in Far Rockaway. Sees his first play in 1923, a melodrama at the Schubert Theatre.

1928   His father's successful manufacturing business in the Garment District, the Miltex Coat and Suit Company, with as many as 800 workers, begins to see hard times faced with the looming Depression. The family moves from Manhattan to rural Brooklyn, where they live at 1350 East 3rd Street, near Avenue M, in the same neighbourhood as his mother's two sisters, Annie Newman and Esther Balsam. Miller plants a pear tree in the backyard ('All I knew was cousins'). Celebrates his bar-mitzvah at the Avenue M Temple.

1930   Transfers from James Madison High School where he is reassigned to the newly built Abraham Lincoln High School on Ocean Parkway. Plays in the football team and injures his leg in a serious accident that will later excuse him from active military service. Academic record unimpressive, and he fails geometry twice.

1931   Early-morning delivery boy for a local bakery before going off to school; forced to stop when his bicycle is stolen. Works for his father during the summer vacation.

1933   Graduates from Abraham Lincoln High School and registers for night school at City College. He leaves after two weeks ('I just couldn't stay awake').

1933– Earns $15 a week as a clerk for Chadwick-
   34   Delamater, an automobile-parts warehouse in a run-
        down section of Manhattan that will later become the site
        for the Lincoln Center for the Performing Arts. He is the
        only Jewish employee, and experiences virulent anti-
        Semitism for the first time.

1934   Writes to the Dean of the University of Michigan to
        appeal against his second rejection and says he has
        become a 'much more serious fellow' ('I still can't believe
        they let me in'). Travels by bus to Ann Arbor for the
        autumn semester, with plans to study journalism because
        'Michigan was one of the few places that took writing
        seriously'. Lives in a rooming house on South Division
        Street and joins the *Michigan Daily* as reporter and night
        editor; takes a non-speaking part in a student production
        of Shakespeare's *King Henry VIII*. Moves to an attic room
        at 411 North State Street and works part-time in an off-
        campus laboratory feeding past-prime vegetables to
        thousands of mice.

1936   Writes his first play, *No Villain*, in six days during semester
        break and receives a Hopwood Award in Drama for $250
        using the pseudonym 'Beyoum'. Changes his major to
        English.

1937   Enrols in Professor Kenneth T. Rowe's playwriting class.
        Rewrites *No Villain* as *They Too Arise* and receives a major
        award of $1,250 from the Theatre Guild's Bureau of New
        Plays (Thomas Lanier – later Tennessee – Williams was
        another winner in the same competition). *They Too Arise* is
        produced by the B'nai Brith Hillel Players in Detroit and
        at the Lydia Mendelssohn Theatre in Ann Arbor.
        Receives a second Hopwood Award for *Honors at Dawn*
        when Susan Glaspell is one of the judges. Contributes to
        The Gargoyle, the student humour magazine. Drives his
        college friend Ralph Neaphus east to join the Abraham
        Lincoln Brigade in the Spanish Civil War, but decides not
        to go with him. Months later Neaphus, twenty-three, was
        dead.

1938   Composes a prison play, *The Great Disobedience*, and revises
        They Too Arise as *The Grass Still Grows*. Graduates from the
        University of Michigan with a BA in English. Joins the
        Federal Theater Project in New York to write radio plays
        and scripts.

1939   The Federal Theater Project is shut down by conservative
       forces in Congress and Miller goes on relief. Writes *Listen
       My Children* and *You're Next* with his friend and fellow
       Michigan alumnus Norman Rosten. *William Ireland's
       Confession* is broadcast on the Columbia Workshop.

1940   Marries Mary Grace Slattery, his college sweetheart at
       the University of Michigan. They move into a small
       apartment at 62 Montague Street in Brooklyn Heights.
       Writes *The Golden Years*, a play about Montezuma, Cortez,
       and the European conquest and corruption of Mexico.
       The Pussycat and the Plumber Who Was a Man airs on CBS
       Radio. Makes a trip to North Carolina to collect dialect
       speech for the Folk Division of the Library of Congress.

1941– Works as a shipfitter's helper on the night shift at the
   43 Brooklyn Navy Yard repairing battle-scarred war vessels
       from the North Atlantic fleet. Finishes additional radio
       plays, including *The Eagle's Nest* and *The Four Freedoms*.
       Completes *The Half-Bridge*. The one-act *That They May Win*
       is produced in New York.

1944   Daughter Jane is born. Prepares Ferenc Molnar's *The
       Guardsman* and Jane Austen's *Pride and Prejudice* for radio
       adaptation, and continues his own writing for the
       medium. Tours army camps in preparation for the draft
       of a screenplay called *The Story of G.I. Joe*, based on news
       reports written by the popular war correspondent Ernie
       Pyle (withdraws from the project when his role as author
       is compromised). Publishes *Situation Normal ...*, a book
       about this experience that highlights the real challenges
       returning soldiers encountered on re-entering civilian life.
       Dedicates the book to his brother, 'Lieutenant Kermit
       Miller, United States Infantry', a war hero. *The Man Who
       Had All the Luck* opens on Broadway but closes after six
       performances, including two previews. The play receives
       the Theater Guild National Award.

1945   Publishes *Focus*, a novel about anti-Semitism and moral
       blindness set in and around New York. His article
       'Should Ezra Pound Be Shot?' appears in *New Masses*.

1946   Adapts *Three Men on a Horse* by George Abbott and John
       C. Holm for radio.

1947   *All My Sons* opens in New York and receives the New
       York Drama Critics' Circle Award; the Donaldson Award
       and the first Tony Award for best author. His son Robert

is born. Moves with his family to a house he purchases at
31 Grace Court in Brooklyn Heights. Also buys a new
car, a Studebaker, and a farmhouse in Roxbury,
Connecticut. Writes the article 'Subsidized Theater' for
the *New York Times*.

1948   Builds by himself a small studio on his Connecticut
property where he writes *Death of a Salesman*. Edward G.
Robinson and Burt Lancaster star in the film version of
All My Sons.

1949   *Death of a Salesman*, starring Lee J. Cobb, Arthur Kennedy,
Cameron Mitchell and Mildred Dunnock, opens at the
Morosco Theatre in New York on 10 February. Directed
by Elia Kazan with designs by Jo Mielziner, it wins the
New York Drama Critics' Circle Award, the Donaldson
Prize, the Antoinette Perry Award, the Theatre Club
Award and the Pulitzer Prize. His essay 'Tragedy and the
Common Man' is printed in the *New York Times*. Attends
the pro-Soviet Cultural and Scientific Conference for
World Peace at the Waldorf-Astoria Hotel to chair a
panel with Clifford Odets and Dimitri Shostakovich.

1950   Adaptation of Henrik Ibsen's *An Enemy of the People* produced
on Broadway starring Fredric March and Florence
Henderson ('I have made no secret of my early love for
Ibsen's work'). First sound recording of *Death of a Salesman*.
The Hook, a film script about graft and corruption in the
closed world of longshoremen in the Red Hook section of
Brooklyn, fails to reach production after backers yield to
pressure from the House Committee on Un-American
Activities. *On the Waterfront*, the Budd Schulberg–Elia Kazan
collaboration featuring Marlon Brando, changes the setting
to Hoboken, New Jersey, but is developed from the same
concept, and is released four years later.

1951   Meets Marilyn Monroe. Fredric March in the role of Willy
Loman for Columbia Pictures in the first film version of
Death of a Salesman. Joseph Buloff translates the play into
Yiddish; his production runs in New York and introduces
Miller's play to Buenos Aires.

1952   Drives to Salem, Massachusetts, and visits the Historical
Society, where he reads documents and researches the
material he will use in *The Crucible*. Breaks with Kazan
over the director's cooperation with HUAC.

1953   *The Crucible* wins the Donaldson Award and the

Antoinette Perry Award when it opens in New York at
the Martin Beck Theatre. Directs *All My Sons* for the
Arden, Delaware, Summer Theatre.

1954   US State Department denies Miller a passport to attend
the Belgian premiere of *The Crucible* in Brussels ('I wasn't
embarrassed for myself; I was embarrassed for my
country'). NBC broadcasts the first radio production of
Death of a Salesman. Mingei Theater stages first Japanese
translation of *Salesman* in Tokyo, where the play is
received as a cautionary tale about the 'salaryman'.

1955   The one-act version of *A View from the Bridge* opens in New
York on a double-bill with *A Memory of Two Mondays*.
HUAC pressurises city officials to withdraw permission
for Miller to make a film about juvenile delinquency set in
New York.

1956   Lives in Nevada for six weeks in order to divorce Mary
Slattery. Marries Marilyn Monroe. Subpoenaed to appear
before HUAC on 21 June, he refuses to name names.
Accepts an honorary degree as Doctor of Humane Letters
from his alma mater, the University of Michigan. Jean-
Paul Sartre writes screenplay for French adaptation of *The
Crucible*, called *Les Sorcieres de Salem*; the film stars Yves
Montand and Simone Signoret. Travels with Monroe to
England, where he meets Laurence Olivier, her co-star in
The Prince and the Showgirl. Peter Brook directs revised two-
act version of *A View from the Bridge* in London at the New
Watergate Theatre Club, as censors determined it could
not be performed in public. 'Once Eddie had been
squarely placed in his social context, among his people,'
Miller noted, 'the myth-like feeling of the story emerged of
itself ... Red Hook is full of Greek tragedies.'

1957   Cited for contempt of Congress for refusing to co-operate
with HUAC. On the steps of the United States Congress,
and with Monroe on his arm, he vows to appeal against
the conviction. Monroe buys all members of Congress a
year's subscription to *I.F. Stone's Weekly*. First television
production of *Death of a Salesman* (ITA, UK). *Arthur Miller's
Collected Plays* is published, and his short story 'The
Misfits' appears in *Esquire Magazine*.

1958– The US Court of Appeals overturns his conviction
59   for contempt of Congress. Elected to the National
Institute of Arts and Letters and receives the Gold Medal
for Drama.

1961   Miller and Monroe divorce (granted in Mexico on the grounds of 'incompatibility'). *The Misfits*, a black-and-white film directed by John Huston featuring the actress in her first serious dramatic role, is released for wide distribution. Miller calls his scenario 'an eastern western' and bases the plot on his short story of the same name. Co-stars include Clark Gable, Montgomery Clift, Eli Wallach and Thelma Ritter. *The Crucible: An Opera in Four Acts* by Robert Ward and Bernard Stambler is recorded. Sidney Lumet directs a movie version of *A View from the Bridge* with Raf Vallone and Carol Lawrence. Miller's mother, Augusta, dies.

1962   Marries Austrian-born Inge Morath, a photographer with Magnum, the agency founded in 1947 by Henri Cartier-Bresson. Marilyn Monroe, aged thirty-six, dies. His daughter, Rebecca Augusta, is born in September. NBC broadcasts an adaptation of *Focus* with James Whitmore and Colleen Dewhurst.

1963   Publishes a children's book, *Jane's Blanket*. Returns to Ann Arbor to deliver annual Hopwood Awards lecture, 'On Recognition'.

1964   Visits the Mauthausen death camp with Inge Morath and covers the Nazi trials in Frankfurt, Germany, for the *New York Herald Tribune*. Reconciles with Kazan. *Incident at Vichy*, whose through-line is 'It's not your guilt I want, it's your responsibility', opens in New York, as does *After the Fall*. The former is the first of the playwright's works to be banned in the Soviet Union. The latter Miller says 'is not about Marilyn' and that she is 'hardly the play's *raison d'etre*'.

1965   Elected president of PEN, the international organisation of writers dedicated to fighting all forms of censorship. American premiere of the two-act version of *A View from the Bridge* is performed Off-Broadway. Laurence Olivier's production of *The Crucible*, starring Colin Blakely and Joyce Redman, is staged in London at the Old Vic by the National Theatre. Returns to Ann Arbor, where his daughter Jane is now a student, to participate in the first teach-in in the US concerning the Vietnam conflict.

1966   First sound recording of *A View from the Bridge*. In Rome Marcello Mastroianni and Monica Vitti play the parts of Quentin and Maggie in Franco Zeffirelli's Italian production of *After the Fall*. Miller's father, Isidore, dies.

1967   *I Don't Need You Any More*, a collection of short stories, is published. Sound recording of *Incident at Vichy*. Television production of *The Crucible* is broadcast on CBS. Visits Moscow and tries to persuade Soviet writers to join PEN. Playwright-in-Residence at the University of Michigan. His son, Daniel, is born in January.

1968   *The Price*, which the playwright called 'a quartet', 'the most specific play I've ever written', opens on Broadway. Sound recording of *After the Fall*. Attends the Democratic National Convention in Chicago as a delegate from Roxbury, Connecticut. Leads peace march against the war in South-East Asia with the Reverend Sloan Coffin, Jr, at Yale University in New Haven. *Death of a Salesman* sells its millionth copy.

1969   *In Russia*, a collaborative project with text by Miller and photography by Morath, is published. Visits Prague in a show of support for Czech writers; meets Vaclav Havel. Retires as president of PEN.

1970   Miller's works are banned in the Soviet Union, a result of his efforts to free dissident writers. *Fame* and *The Reason Why*, two one-act plays, are produced; the latter is filmed at his home in Connecticut.

1971   Television productions of *A Memory of Two Mondays* on PBS and *The Price* on NBC. Sound recording of *An Enemy of the People*. *The Portable Arthur Miller* is published.

1972   *The Creation of the World and Other Business* opens at the Schubert Theatre in New York on 30 November. Attends the Democratic National Convention in Miami as a delegate. First sound recording of *The Crucible*.

1973   PBS broadcasts Stacy Keach's television adaptation of *Incident at Vichy*, with Harris Yulin as Leduc. Champions the case of Peter Reilly, an eighteen-year-old falsely convicted of manslaughter for his mother's murder; four years later, all charges are dismissed. *After the Fall* with Faye Dunaway is televised on NBC. Teaches mini-course at the University of Michigan; students perform early drafts of scenes from *The American Clock*.

1974   *Up from Paradise*, musical version of *The Creation of the World and Other Business*, is staged at the Power Center for the Performing Arts at the University of Michigan. With music by Stanley Silverman and cover design by Al Hirschfield, Miller calls it his 'heavenly cabaret'.

1977   A second collaborative project with Inge Morath, *In the Country*, is published. Petitions the Czech government to halt arrests of dissident writers. The *Archbishop's Ceiling* opens at the Kennedy Center in Washington, DC. Miller said he wanted to dramatise 'what happens … when people know they are … at all times talking to Power, whether through a bug or a friend who really is an informer'.

1978   *The Theater Essays of Arthur Miller* is published. NBC broadcasts the film of *Fame* starring Richard Benjamin. Belgian National Theatre mounts the twenty-fifth anniversary production of *The Crucible*; this time Miller can attend.

1979   *Chinese Encounters*, with Inge Morath, is published. Michael Rudman directs a major revival of *Death of a Salesman* at the National Theatre in London, with Warren Mitchell as Willy Loman.

1980   *Playing for Time*, the film based on Fania Fenelon's autobiography *The Musicians of Auschwitz*, is broadcast nationally on CBS, with Vanessa Redgrave and Jane Alexander. ('I tried to treat it as a story meaningful to the survivors, by which I mean all of us. I didn't want it to be a mere horror story.') *The American Clock* has its first performance at the Spoleto Festival in South Carolina, then opens in New York with the playwright's sister, Joan Copeland, as Rose Baum, a role based on their mother. Miller sees his play as 'a mural', 'a mosaic', 'a story of America talking to itself … There's never been a society that hasn't had a clock running on it, and you can't help wondering – How long?'

1981   Second volume of *Arthur Miller's Collected Plays* is published. Delivers keynote address on the fiftieth anniversary of the Hopwood Awards Program in Ann Arbor.

1982   Two one-act plays that represent 'the colors of memory', *Elegy for a Lady* and *Some Kind of Love Story*, are produced as a double-bill at the Long Wharf Theatre in Connecticut under the title *2 by A.M.*

1983   Directs *Death of a Salesman* at the People's Art Theatre in Beijing, part of a cultural exchange to mark the early stage of the opening of diplomatic relations between the United States and the People's Republic of China. Ying Ruocheng plays Willy Loman in his own Chinese

translation. *I Think About You a Great Deal*, a monologue
written as a tribute to Vaclav Havel, appears in *Cross
Currents*, University of Michigan.

1984   *'Salesman' in Beijing* is published. The texts of *Elegy for a
Lady* and *Some Kind of Love Story* are printed under a new
title, *Two-Way Mirror*. Receives Kennedy Center Honors
for lifetime achievement. Reworks the script of *The
American Clock* for Peter Wood's London production at the
National Theatre.

1985   Twenty-five million viewers see Dustin Hoffman play
Willy Loman, with John Malkovich as Biff and Kate Reid
as Linda in the production of *Death of a Salesman* shown on
CBS. Goes to Turkey with Harold Pinter for PEN as an
ambassador for freedom of speech. Serves as delegate at a
meeting of Soviet and American writers in Vilnius,
Lithuania, where he attacks Russian authorities for their
continuing anti-Semitism and persecution of *samizdat*
writers. *The Archbishop's Ceiling* is produced in the UK by
the Bristol Old Vic. Completes adaptation of *Playing for
Time* as a stage play.

1986   One of fifteen writers and scientists invited to meet
Mikhail Gorbachev to discuss Soviet policies. The Royal
Shakespeare Company uses a revised script of *The
Archbishop's Ceiling* for its London production in the
Barbican Pit.

1987   Miller publishes *Timebends: A Life*, his autobiography.
Characterising it as 'a preemptive strike' against future
chroniclers, he discusses his relationship with Marilyn
Monroe in public for the first time. *Clara* and *I Can't
Remember Anything* open as a double-bill at Lincoln Center
in New York under the title *Danger: Memory!* Broadcasts of
The Golden Years on BBC Radio and Jack O'Brien's
television production of *All My Sons* on PBS. Michael
Gambon stars as Eddie Carbone in Alan Ayckbourn's
intimate production of *A View from the Bridge* at the
National Theatre in London. University of East Anglia
names its site for American Studies the Arthur Miller
Centre.

1988   Publishes 'Waiting for the Teacher', a nineteen-stanza free-
verse poem, in *Ha'aretz*, the Tel Aviv-based liberal
newspaper, on the occasion of the fiftieth anniversary of the
founding of the State of Israel.

1990   *Everybody Wins*, directed by Karel Reisz with Debra Winger and Nick Nolte, is released: 'Through the evolution of the story – a murder that took place before the story opens – we will be put through an exercise in experiencing reality and unreality.' Television production of *An Enemy of the People* on PBS. Josette Simon plays Maggie as a sultry jazz singer in Michael Blakemore's London revival of *After the Fall* at the National Theatre, where *The Crucible* also joins the season's repertory in Howard Davies's production starring Zoë Wannamaker and Tom Wilkinson. Updated version of *The Man Who Had All the Luck* is staged by Paul Unwin in a joint production by the Bristol Old Vic and the Young Vic in London.

1991   *The Last Yankee* premieres as a one-act play. *The Ride Down Mount Morgan*, 'a moral farce', has its world premiere in London: 'The play is really a kind of nightmare.' Television adaptation of *Clara* on the Arts & Entertainment Network. Receives Mellon Bank Award for lifetime achievement in the humanities.

1992   *Homely Girl, A Life* is published with artwork by Louise Bourgeois in a Peter Blum edition. Writes satirical op-ed piece for the *New York Times* urging an end to capital punishment in the US.

1993   Expanded version of *The Last Yankee* opens at the Manhattan Theatre Club in New York. Television version of *The American Clock* on TNT with the playwright's daughter, Rebecca, in the role of Edie.

1994   *Broken Glass*, a work 'full of ambiguities' that takes 'us back to the time when the social contract was being torn up', has a pre-Broadway run at the Long Wharf Theatre in Connecticut; opens at the Booth Theatre in New York on 24 April. David Thacker's London production wins the Olivier Award for Best Play.

1995   Tributes to the playwright on the occasion of his eightieth birthday are held in England and the US. Receives William Inge Festival Award for Distinguished Achievement in American Theater. *Homely Girl, A Life and Other Stories* is published. In England the collection appears under the title *Plain Girl*. Darryl V. Jones directs a production of *A View from the Bridge* in Washington, DC, and resets the play in a community of Domincan immigrants. The Arthur Miller Society is founded by Steve Centola.

1996   Revised and expanded edition of *The Theater Essays of Arthur Miller* is published. Receives the Edward Albee Last Frontier Playwright Award. Rebecca Miller and Daniel Day-Lewis are married.

1997   *The Crucible*, produced by the playwright's son, Robert A. Miller, is released for wide distribution and is nominated for an Academy Award. Revised version of *The Ride Down Mount Morgan* performed at the Williamstown Playhouse in Massachusetts. BBC airs television version of *Broken Glass*, with Margot Leicester and Henry Goodman repeating their roles from the award-winning London production.

1998   *Mr Peters' Connections* opens in New York with Peter Falk. Revival of *A View from the Bridge* by the Roundabout Theatre Company wins two Tony Awards. Revised version of *The Ride Down Mount Morgan* on Broadway. Miller is named Distinguished Inaugural Senior Fellow of the American Academy in Berlin.

1999   Robert Falls's fiftieth anniversary production of *Death of a Salesman*, featuring Brian Dennehy as Willy Loman, moves from the Goodman Theater in Chicago and opens on Broadway, where it wins the Tony Award for Best Revival of a Play. Co-authors the libretto with Arnold Weinstein for William Bolcom's opera of *A View from the Bridge*, which has its world premiere at the Lyric Opera of Chicago.

2000   Patrick Stewart reprises his role as Lyman Felt in *The Ride Down Mount Morgan* on Broadway, where *The Price* is also revived (with Harris Yulin). Major eighty-fifth birthday celebrations are organised by Christopher Bigsby at the University of East Anglia and by Enoch Brater at the University of Michigan, where plans are announced to build a new theatre named in his honour; it opens officially on 29 March 2007 ('whoever thought when I was saving $500 to come to the University of Michigan that it would come to this'). 'Up to a certain point the human being is completely unpredictable. That's what keeps me going ... You live long enough, you don't rust.' *Echoes Down the Corridor*, a collection of essays from 1944 to 2000, is published. Miller and Morath travel to Cuba with William and Rose Styron and meet Fidel Castro and the Colombian writer Gabriel García Márquez.

2001   Williamstown Theater Festival revives *The Man Who Had All the Luck*. Laura Dern and William H. Macy star in a film based on the 1945 novel *Focus*. Miller is named the Jefferson Lecturer in the Humanities by NEH and receives the John H. Finley Award for Exemplary Service to New York City. His speech *On Politics and the Art of Acting* is published.

2002   Revivals in New York of *The Man Who Had All the Luck* and *The Crucible*, the latter with Liam Neeson as John Proctor. *Resurrection Blues* has its world premiere at the Guthrie Theatre in Minneapolis. Miller receives a major international award in Spain, the Premio Principe de Asturias de las Letras. Death of Inge Morath.

2003   Awarded the Jerusalem Prize. His brother, Kermit Miller, dies on 17 October. *The Price* is performed at the Tricycle Theatre in London.

2004   *Finishing the Picture* opens at the Goodman Theatre in Chicago. *After the Fall* revived in New York. Appears on a panel at the University of Michigan with Mark Lamos, who directs students in scenes from Miller's rarely performed plays.

2005   Miller dies of heart failure in his Connecticut home on 10 February. Public memorial service is held on 9 May at the Majestic Theatre in New York, with 1,500 in attendance. Asked what he wanted to be remembered for, the playwright said, 'A few good parts for actors.'

Plot

In the first of the play's two scenes, Leroy Hamilton and
John Frick meet in a waiting room of the large state mental
hospital where their wives are patients. The room's windows
look out over a large parking lot and the hospital grounds.
At the beginning of the second scene, the action shifts to
Patricia Hamilton's hospital room and part of an adjoining
recreation space. Patricia shares her room with an unnamed
woman who spends the entire scene lying quietly on one of
the beds. The play takes place on one day, and the first
scene overlaps the beginning of the second in time; Patricia
Hamilton and Karen Frick talk in the hospital ward as their
husbands talk in the waiting room. Once Leroy enters the
second scene, Karen leaves the stage until she and her
husband rejoin the Hamiltons towards the play's end.

Scene One
Leroy Hamilton sits in an empty waiting room, reading a
magazine, with a banjo case at his feet. When John Frick
enters, he betrays far more impatience than the younger
man and asks Leroy's advice about the hospital's visiting
routine. Leroy, still calm, would be glad to be left to himself,
but Frick, obviously anxious, repeatedly draws Leroy into
conversation about the hospital, its patients and, not
incidentally, his own prejudices. Frick first points out the
hospital's vast parking lot, which Leroy assures him actually
fills up with visiting families and friends at weekends. Frick
has his doubts but he also concedes that, walking outside, he
cannot tell the difference between patients and visitors just
by looking at them. Frick clearly finds his wife's illness
perplexing and his behaviour also shows his embarrassment
at using a public mental hospital for his wife's care,

particularly when he could afford a more exclusive, private (and, he suggests, less racially diverse) facility. Leroy surprises Frick when he says that this is his wife's third admission and that she's been in the hospital for seven weeks already. He admits that he could take Patricia home now but does not feel ready to do so.

Much of Leroy and Frick's initial conversation revolves around clinical depression, a topic neither seems to understand. Both men search for common ground, but their conversation shows how far apart their lives are. Leroy and Patricia Hamilton have seven children; the Fricks have none. The Fricks have money; the Hamiltons pinch pennies. Patricia Hamilton is beautiful; Karen Frick is plain. Neither woman works outside the home, but to hear their husbands describe it, both women eventually saw their homes as shelters and then as prisons, refusing to go out at all. The men start to talk about the domestic responsibilities each has taken on, and about the sadness that sometimes threatens them, too. As they continue to compare notes, Frick wonders if being an only child has contributed to Karen's sadness. Leroy then begins to complain about Patricia's siblings, who, he says, are ashamed to see their sister in a 'public institution' (9).

Both Leroy and Frick describe the Rogers Pavilion, a private hospital some distance away. Frick could afford to send Karen there if he wanted to but claims to prefer the hospital his taxes pay for. His feelings are obviously conflicted, however, because his subsequent descriptions of the Rogers Pavilion make it clear that he admires the white, upper-class values it represents. Leroy admits Patricia's family would pay the Rogers' high fees, but he prefers the state hospital. Miller's stage directions indicate that this disclosure matters to Leroy and, initially, Frick admires his pride. From this compliment, however, their rapport quickly descends into rancour as Frick begins to complain about those who take handouts, conflating them with a plumber he believes overcharged him for a simple job. When Frick quotes the plumber's $17 hourly rate, Leroy visibly bristles. Frick asks Leroy what kind of work he does, reacting with shock when Leroy reveals that he is a carpenter. The tension in the room increases as Frick tries to explain why he thought that the well-dressed, well-spoken Leroy must have worked in a higher-status position. Frick, who once owned a lumberyard, has not recognised one of his former customers. When Frick learns Leroy's full name, he remembers reading a newspaper article about him and his famous ancestor, Alexander Hamilton, one of America's Founding Fathers. Frick, obsessed with outward appearances, claims he would have recognised Leroy had he been wearing his work clothes and asks how much money he makes. Leroy answers $17 an hour and Frick, ironically, is quick to say that he should charge as much as the market will bear.

During this opening exchange, Frick can say nothing right. Every compliment he tries to make insults Leroy and every assumption he speaks betrays a world-view Leroy finds revolting. On the one hand, he admires an altar Leroy has just completed for a local church, but then he also makes it clear that for a man of his distinguished ancestry, a mere trade like carpentry seems both unexpected and demeaning, as if, of course, selling lumber, although more lucrative, was an exalted profession. When Leroy admits his father was a lawyer, Frick becomes even more confused, since he now sees Leroy's life as a downward slide. If life in America is supposed to be all about upward mobility and the American Dream, Leroy, in Frick's opinion, has taken a very bad turn. Frick begins to talk to Leroy with condescension, unaware that Leroy might have his own opinions on Alexander Hamilton's philosophy and at the same time not believing that his father might have hated being a lawyer. Leroy finally snaps, telling Frick that 'this whole kind of conversation' (14) might be why there are so many patients to fill the state mental hospital. Frick, still not understanding how he has managed to offend Leroy, returns to the window, and the lights go down on both men, still waiting to be called into the hospital's interior rooms.

Scene Two

The second scene opens inside the hospital ward, and the
audience sees Patricia's room and part of a Recreation
Room to one side. Initially, the only person on stage is the
unnamed Patient, lying on a bed. She will remain on stage
for the rest of the play although the other characters ignore
her completely. In comparison, Patricia Hamilton and
Karen Frick, who have been playing ping-pong just offstage,
seem particularly animated even as they stop their game.
From the outset, Patricia takes the lead in their
conversations, while the older Karen alternates between
following her lead and falling into her own confused
thoughts. The pattern they establish mimics their husbands'
conversation outside this space: the anxious Karen peppers
the higher-functioning Patricia with questions; and,
flattered, she allows herself to be drawn into the
conversation. Patricia's answers detail how she perceives the
hospital and she quickly suggests to Karen that keeping her
husband waiting might be a good thing. Like Leroy, Patricia
is uncertain about when it would be safe to go home, and
she asks Karen not to tell anyone – doctors included – that
she has now gone three weeks without taking any
medication.

Karen's *non sequiturs* make for good exposition as they skip
from drugs to religion to hunting to lawsuits to Patricia's
good looks. Patricia, who clearly hides information from her
doctors, finds Karen reassuring to talk to, precisely because
she 'probably won't remember too much' (18). Karen and
Patricia touch on many of the themes their husbands are
discussing in the waiting room: the nature of depression,
people's tendency to judge by appearances, Yankee values.
Patricia's and Karen's status as patients lets them question
things people normally take for granted. The hospital setting
allows patients and visitors to ask questions, waiting for
answers and connections previously unacknowledged.

The problems in the Hamiltons' relationship may have a
lot to do with Patricia's depression, but it soon becomes
evident that Patricia disagrees with Leroy in some of the
same ways as Frick does. She despairs that he allows himself

to be taken advantage of, and that he is not motivated by her version of the American Dream and the mad rush to get ahead in life. Success to Patricia means money and the things money can buy. When she sees that Karen, who clearly has money, has also been paralysed by depression, Patricia must re-examine her own life as well as her marriage. Both women repeatedly return to the mundane, commercial aspects of life – what cars to drive, where to shop for groceries, or whether to grow vegetables in the yard. Each seems to want what the other takes for granted and both women act surprised by what the other desires. Patricia feels betrayed when Leroy talks of donating his antique tools to a museum, rather than keeping them as things of value, perhaps for later sale. She also finds Leroy's banjo-playing inappropriate, and she resents the money he spends on music lessons. Karen, who has taken up tap-dance, would love to be married to a banjo player.

Despite their differences, Patricia's and Karen's illnesses allow them – and the audience – to see what they have in common. For example, both women seem haunted by their mothers; Patricia's died two years earlier, and Karen thinks she hears her mother moving around in the next room when she is alone at home. Karen admits freely, however, that her family was not at all close; Patricia remembers that hers was. She describes how beautiful her relatives were, tall, blond Swedes, and how her mother and sisters would sunbathe nude on the roof of their house. Her brothers were both handsome and athletic; one was even an Olympic pole-vaulter. Both brothers, however, committed suicide within eight days of one another. Karen asks why, and Patricia says both were disappointed that life was not going to turn out to be what they had been brought up to believe. On this sombre note, Karen decides to join her waiting husband and Leroy takes her place in Patricia's room.

Alone, the Hamiltons approach each other cautiously while replaying a dialogue they appear to have had many times before. Leroy notices that Patricia seems more vibrant today, but shows his disappointment when she refuses to confide in him. Both are tense with expectation and each

wants the conversation to go better than it does. While
Patricia holds back her surprise for Leroy, he tells her that
he has negotiated a higher price for the altar he has just
completed for the Presbyterian church, which she had been
eager for him to do. She reacts at first by taking the credit
for pushing him to ask for more money but then pulls back,
praising him for making his own decision. In exchange,
Leroy wants Patricia to tell him what has changed about her
condition. She recoils when he credits the doctors for her
improvement and he carefully relents. When he mentions
the possibility of buying a new oil burner from Frick, she
exults that she might come home soon. This brings their
awkward *pas de deux* to a climax of sorts as, with great care,
they focus on what her illness means to each of them and
what it might mean to move past it now.

Patricia makes it clear that she believes Leroy is even
more depressed than she is. Leroy holds himself up as a
realist, arguing that he reacts to the world around him as it
is now, while his wife, in his opinion, cannot shake herself
loose from the burden of history. She does not want to hear
how her own father thought that no Yankee – even Leroy –
was worthy of his daughter, or how prosperous Swedish
families are today. Leroy, on the other hand, always tries to
dismiss the past as irrelevant. He complains that a man he
once hired to help him stole tools, despite being from a
respected local family with a distinguished history. Patricia
claims that she suffers when Leroy denies his own problems;
but, through the case of her brothers, he has already seen
what happens when expectations inflate themselves beyond
reason. Goaded, he retaliates by bringing up her brothers'
suicides; it seems as though they will never escape this
escalating cycle of misery. Patricia sees the necessity now of
looking only a little way into the future, while Leroy
constantly tries to drag both of them out of the past. At the
same time, Leroy understands that they are not the only
ones to be ensnared by an American Dream gone sour. He
wants to live an honest life, full of craft and family and fresh
air, but those around him – Patricia, Frick – refuse to see
that as another and more vibrant form of success.

As they talk, Patricia and Leroy ricochet between their current situation and the larger story of their life. Earlier, Patricia blamed Karen's incoherence on the medication, but even though she has been free from drugs for three weeks, Patricia herself still jumps from place to place, asking Leroy to discuss different aspects of their relationship, drawing new lines between the present and the past. She really wants to know how she has managed, after all this time, not to drive him away. He hates seeing her do this to herself but, at the same time, he admits that but for their seven children, he might have left. They return, again, to debate the virtues of reality versus idealism, physical pleasure versus spiritual exploration, settling for things versus striving for more. This round ends in a draw, with Patricia deciding not to leave the hospital today and Leroy offering to play his new banjo number before leaving for his lesson. The banjo frames the last elements of their conflict before the Fricks return to the stage.

Now, for the first time, all five characters inhabit the stage space together (the unnamed Patient still lies on a bed). Karen, despite seeming the least articulate of the four, manages the introductions. Frick, who has brought Karen's tap-dance costume, dithers between appreciating Karen's animation and his mortification at her desire to perform in satin shorts and a top hat. While Karen moves offstage, Frick praises Patricia for restoring Karen's interest in the world around her. Leroy seems dumbstruck to hear Patricia dispense his own advice to someone else while seeming to ignore it herself. Patricia then lectures Frick on how to approach his wife, warning that he must not betray any sense of disappointment. Frick then turns to Leroy, remarking that he, too, 'could do with some of [Patricia's] optimism' (42). While Leroy tries to regain his bearings, Patricia questions Frick closely about Karen's habit of tap dancing in the basement in the middle of the night. He admits that Karen's dancing not only disturbs his sense of order, but claims it interferes with his ability to run his businesses. Leroy, who has previously lost all patience with Frick in the first scene, rather enjoys watching the older man being run roughshod by Patricia. Earlier, Patricia castigated Leroy for refusing to make money but, faced with Frick, she suggests that Frick's dogged focus on his work has landed his wife in the hospital.

When Karen returns, in costume, she asks her husband to sing 'Swanee River' for her to dance to. Frick at first objects but then gives in, weakly singing about being happy 'far, far away'. The Hamiltons praise Karen and encourage Frick to appreciate her performance, but Patricia's exuberance perhaps goes too far. Frick loses his composure, shouting, 'I am looking at her, goddammit!' (44) Karen, frightened, tries to smooth over the social awkwardness, while Frick apologises for his outburst and tries to leave. Karen intercepts him and Frick tries awkwardly to put Patricia's lesson into words, doing his best to make sure Karen does not suffer under the weight of his disappointment. Clearly, his best is not enough and he abruptly leaves the stage.

Karen, who had previously danced well, now finds herself nearly paralysed as Patricia moves to reassure her. Patricia asks Leroy to play the song on his banjo so that Karen can dance again. After a few bars, Karen asks him to play a bit faster while she takes a tentative step or two, but she cannot sustain the performance any longer. Once Leroy stops playing, she, too, walks out of the room. The Hamiltons, left to themselves, enact a quiet moment of decision. Patricia begins to pack her things and they both make ready to walk out of the hospital together. Their previous arguments give way to a mutual generosity of spirit, and they speak affectionately to each other as they leave the stage, while the unnamed Patient remains on the bed behind them.

Commentary

Themes

The Last Yankee highlights conflicts between men and
women, between the working class and those who have left
manual labour behind, and between appearances and
realities. Set in a New England state mental hospital in the
early 1990s, the play creates spaces in which the four
characters, in shifting pairs, grapple with definitions of
sanity and success. Early in the second scene, Patricia
Hamilton and Karen Frick make a wide survey of mental
illness and their own lives as their husbands had previously
examined class conflict and material gain in the outside
world. Karen's medicated state contrasts with Patricia's
conviction that psychotropic drugs are dangerous. Once the
husbands join them on stage, the play attacks the barriers
that separate the patients from the visitors. Miller was
concerned with the social symbolism of clinical depression,
which, 'far from being merely a question of an individual's
illness', can show us what we really mean by happiness and
by success. *The Last Yankee* was written in the early days of
the Prozac revolution, when the idea of a quick, chemical fix
to both ordinary sadness and social oppression captivated
many Americans.

The characters in *The Last Yankee* debate many aspects of
the American Dream, a national mythology of striving for
success. Leroy Hamilton and John Frick illustrate the
tensions between the skilled craftsman and the capitalist
who will pursue any form of business if the bottom line
makes sense. Inside the state mental hospital, Patricia
Hamilton and Karen Frick critique both husbands' choices
as they try to find their way through cultural and personal
miasma, what Miller, in his essay 'About Theatre
Language', called 'the moral and social myths feeding the

disease'. 'The main thing I sought in *The Last Yankee*,' Miller wrote,

> was to make real my sense of the life of such people, the kind of man swinging the hammer through a lifetime, the kind of woman waiting forever for her ship to come in. And second, my view of their present confusion and, if you will, decay and possible recovery. They are bedrock, aspiring not to greatness but to other gratifications – successful parenthood, decent children and a decent house and a decent car and an occasional nice evening with family or friends, and above all, of course, some financial security. Needless to say, they are people who can be inspired to great and noble sacrifice, but also to bitter hatreds. As the world goes I suppose they are the luckiest people, but some of them – a great many, in fact – have grown ill with what would once have been called a sickness of the soul.

The social nature of 'soul sickness', the individual's responsibilities for the well-being of the community as a whole, mattered deeply to Miller. Just as he established his theatrical mastery in *Death of a Salesman* by calling attention to the tragedy of the common man, towards the end of his career he kept his focus firmly on those whom America's 'success mythology' would often have us forget.

While those outside the United States may use the word Yankee to refer to any American, to be a Yankee in the context of the play is to be a New Englander, specifically one whose family had not recently arrived from any other country (such as, in this case, Sweden). The word implies a white, Anglo-Saxon, Protestant heritage, a preference for plain talk and a penchant for everyday common sense. The Revolutionary War-era song 'Yankee Doodle' pokes fun at a rag-tag rebel who 'stuck a feather in his cap and called it macaroni'. Despite its satirical origins, Yankee is a label most in the region wear with pride and 'Yankee Doodle' is the official state song, for example, of Connecticut, one of the original thirteen colonies that later became the United States of America.

What's in a name?

Leroy Hamilton's name carries mixed messages. His first
name, Leroy, although derived from the French for 'the
king', carries plebian and rural connotations in modern
American usage. In contrast, Miller's use of Alexander
Hamilton as Leroy's famous ancestor, raises many
suggestive points, not least of which is the contrast between
'Leroy' and 'Alexander', as the latter suggests the empire-
building of Alexander the Great. Alexander Hamilton is one
of the most famous American 'Founding Fathers', a
distinguished group comprising the Signers, the men who
signed the Declaration of Independence in 1776, and the
Framers, who drafted the United States Constitution.
Hamilton, as a result of his political and economic
philosophies, his fiery temper and perhaps his
unconventional biography, remains one of the most
controversial of the American founders. He is also
remembered for his notorious death: in 1801, Vice-
President Aaron Burr killed him in a duel. Today his
portrait appears on the American ten-dollar bill. Leroy
and Frick briefly allude to Hamilton in the first scene
of *The Last Yankee*, when Leroy's reluctance to take
pride in his lineage perplexes Frick the self-made
businessman.

During the American Revolutionary War, Hamilton
served George Washington, the first American president, as
a trusted aide in matters both strategic and diplomatic and
he later served as Secretary of the Treasury in Washington's
administration. Politically, Hamilton advocated both a
strong central government and an industrial economy for
the new country. He clashed repeatedly with Thomas
Jefferson and other founders who argued in favour of
decentralised political power and the primacy of an agrarian
society. His greatest contribution to American political
philosophy, *The Federalist Papers*, co-written with John Jay
and James Madison, formed part of his effort to have the
new American Constitution ratified by the states. As
Treasury Secretary, Hamilton mapped out institutions and
initiatives that would shape the American market economy

for centuries to come, emphasising industry, trade and banking.

Miller is not the first American writer to use Alexander Hamilton to comment on materialism and the growing influence of business in American life. The twentieth-century New Jersey poet William Carlos Williams derided Hamilton's capitalist ambitions for the country, particularly his involvement in the Society for the Establishment of Useful Manufactures, a corporation that planned to harness the power of New Jersey's Passaic River, including its stunning waterfalls, for industrial use. In his poems collected in *Paterson* and *In the American Grain*, Williams, himself a socialist, often sneered at Hamilton, calling him 'a type that needed power'.

While *The Last Yankee*'s title calls more immediate attention to Hamilton's last name, Miller emphasises Frick's surname by using it in the speech headings. The name Frick comes with a complex history of its own. Henry Clay Frick was a hugely successful American capitalist in the late nineteenth and early twentieth century. He was Andrew Carnegie's partner in the businesses that would one day become US Steel. Although his grandfather was a successful whisky distiller in western Pennsylvania, Henry Clay Frick grew up in relative poverty. John Frick, too, exposes his humble roots, revealing that he 'started from down below sea level myself, sixty acres of rocks and swampland is all we had' (41).

Henry Clay Frick educated himself in business and soon began to build an empire of coke smelters in western Pennsylvania. Fiercely anti-union from early in his career, Frick took the lead in breaking the Amalgamated Association of Iron and Steel Workers at Homestead, Pennsylvania, one of the deadliest clashes between workers and owners in America's labour history. Whereas Andrew Carnegie often espoused pro-union positions, Frick had no use for labour's interference in business, and Carnegie made sure he was out of the country when Frick drove the Homestead crisis to its bloody climax. In response to workers occupying the factories, Frick sent in three hundred armed Pinkerton guards; several workers died in the ensuing clash. The Homestead Strike marks the moment in American labour history when unions of skilled craftspeople, not unlike Leroy Hamilton, crumbled before the demands of the corporate managers of modern industrialisation. Henry Clay Frick is mostly remembered today, however, as the founder of the famous Frick Collection of art and artifacts in New York, located in what was once his elegant Manhattan residence on East 70th Street and Fifth Avenue.

Another famous Frick was a Nazi. Wilhelm Frick served as Adolph Hitler's interior minister from 1933 to 1943, and helped to draft the notorious Nuremberg race laws. Enacted in September 1935, the Nuremberg laws stripped German Jews of their citizenship, forbade sexual relations between Jews and gentile German citizens, and laid down the criteria by which the Third Reich would determine a person's Jewish identity. A lawyer with a bureaucrat's penchant for orderly systems, Wilhelm Frick was tried for crimes against humanity by the International Military Tribunal at Nuremberg. He was executed in 1946.

Tranquility and tranquilisers

The use of pharmacology to treat depression is a late-twentieth-century phenomenon. The first drug widely used to treat depression did not make its appearance until the 1950s. There followed a succession of other drugs with various drawbacks and side-effects. In 1987 Prozac was approved for use. Prozac differed from its predecessors in that it specifically focused on serotonin, the substance that regulates mood in the brain. Its function was to stabilise serotonin levels without affecting other systems or creating dangerous side-effects. It was instantly popular. However, soon it was reported that Prozac created increased compulsions towards violent and suicidal behaviour in some patients; a study published in the *American Journal of Psychiatry* also concluded that patients suffering these effects improved when they stopped taking the drug.

In *The Last Yankee*, Miller adds his voice to those who

doubted its safety and efficacy. Part of Miller's objection has to be practical; depression makes an inferior symbol for what ails American society if it can be cured by simply taking a pill. As Patricia, in a moment of piety, reminds Karen, 'the soul belongs to God, we're not supposed to be stuffing Prozac into his mouth' (19). With her long history of illness and treatment, Patricia chooses to leave pharmaceuticals behind at a time when millions of Americans, who had never before considered anti-depressants, were starting to taking them.

Karen, who has been admitted to the hospital after an overdose of pills, takes even more of them once inside. Her moments of happiness come only briefly when she dances with *'joyous freedom'* (44). The pills, however, do not drive her to dance; Karen brings her love of dance with her. Through this example, Miller shows how drugs like Prozac threaten the one emotional outlet Karen has. As Patricia observes, 'the minute they see you enjoying yourself they'll probably try to knock you out with a pill' (25). Leroy, *The Last Yankee*'s title character, has always argued the superior efficacy of fresh air and an honest day's work. On stage, the audience sees Patricia most fully embrace her recovery at the moment she comes to agree with him.

The hospital as crucible
The Last Yankee's hospital setting would seem to focus the audience's attention on the individual patients, their illnesses and the care they receive. The hospital creates a defined space, separate from daily life, where people can say things that cannot be said elsewhere. Miller's hospital becomes a place from which his characters observe and critique the world outside. Inside this public asylum, Karen Frick can bring her tap-dancing out of the basement just as Patricia Hamilton, separated from her husband and their many children, can commandeer her own treatment. The two scenes of *The Last Yankee* explore the significance of women's mental illness on the stage, first as a meeting-place for the men, and then as a space the women inhabit. Temporarily

separated from the outside world, Karen and Patricia use
the state mental hospital as a laboratory for social
experiment. The hospital acts as a crucible in which patients
refine and distil the social causes of their distress. It is a stage
upon which patients have the possibility of changing
themselves before emerging to change everything else.

Although *The Last Yankee* establishes many aspects of the
hospital setting – a waiting room, a patient in bed, talk of
unseen gatekeepers – hospitals represent illness as well as the
pursuit of health; they evoke both birth and death and many
stages in between. As social institutions, they are places of
violation as well as care. Society may claim to value the
privacy of medical information, but within hospital walls,
privacy is compromised; very little of the body or the mind
remains hidden for long. Hospitals function according to
their own rules, often incomprehensible to outsiders.

Hospitals concentrate patients in therapeutic
environments where physicians and caregivers are best able
to treat them, relieving families and communities of the
burden of caring for their sickest members. A hospital, like a
prison, also functions as an instrument of social control; it is
the place where the ill, the weak and the deviant may be
isolated from the general population. These cultural images
cannot be considered separately. In *The Last Yankee*, no
doctors are present. Patricia Hamilton mentions a Dr
Rockwell, who appears to be easily deceived, and Karen
Frick's over-medicated state casts doubts on her physician's
competence. In their absence Miller concentrates instead on
the role of the hospital or asylum as a place where personal
and social crises can be represented and examined.

Staging anxiety – a female focus
In several of Miller's late plays, mental illness is assumed to
have roots in the characters' behaviour and moral nature,
and in the texture of their daily lives. This enables the plays'
characters to make judgements about the social forces they
see as intricately linked to their situation on stage. Illness
becomes the catalyst that empowers the two women in the

play to comment on the world around them at the same time as they are free to resist its oppressive forces, even actual psychiatric treatment.

Inside *The Last Yankee*'s hospital, the patients expose their own sets of definitions and assumptions about mental illness. Karen, struggling to understand her own predicament, jumps from topic to topic as Patricia's conversation sparks her memories about the past. Although she has been eager to discuss her husband's hunting, grocery stores and General Motors and her mother, she has always avoided the state of her own feelings in these discussions. Early in the second scene she recognises images of the world that circumscribe her life. After many years of struggling with depression, Patricia has come to see her illness in its social context, and she sees herself as soldier in the army of the oppressed, arguing that 'anybody with any sense has got to be depressed in this country' (22). Karen admires Patricia for her ability, as well as her audacity, to analyse the world around her, which is something that Karen has not yet learned to do.

For the patients in *The Last Yankee* to have any hope of recovery, the boundaries of the institution must be permeable. Miller's asylum is not merely a sanctuary or a warehouse; it is a laboratory where the connections between public and private life can be examined, nurtured, and finally understood. In this play, rooted in conflicting expressions of the American Dream, characters seek out the hospital's neutral space in an attempt to effect change not only within individuals, but between them. Entry into the asylum does not guarantee success, however; there are three patients in this hospital and they represent a range of situations and of possibilities.

In contrast both to Patricia, who has reached a stage in her illness where she actively pursues health, and to Karen, just beginning to heal with Patricia's help, the first character the audience sees at the beginning of the play's second act *'lies motionless with one arm over her eyes'*. The opening stage directions indicate that *'she will not move throughout the scene'* (15). She is a comatose 'unnamed patient'. Reading the text

that follows, she is easy to forget, but like the body on the
bed in the second act of Edward Albee's *Three Tall Women*
(1991), she commands the audience's attention in the
theatre. She does not move, and she represents the worst-
case scenario in this ward of sidelined women, a depressive
beyond the reach of any social interaction. Her paralysis
represents what the others characters fear. In a play where
two couples have each been separated by an inability to
communicate at the most rudimentary human levels, she
reminds the characters and the audience that no amount of
psychiatry or degree of social change may be able to restore
health or intimacy completely. At the play's end, at least one
patient on stage is trapped in an image of madness, beyond
the reach of therapy. Patricia tells Karen in the second
scene that more people are hospitalised for depression than
for any other disease. What she doesn't say, the men have
already implied: in the United States, women experience
major depressive episodes at almost twice the rate of men,
and the numbers are similar for most affective anxiety
disorders.

Genre

The Last Yankee brings to conclusion Miller's experiments
with one-act plays. Following two double-bills (*Elegy for a
Lady* and *Some Kind of Love Story*, performed together as *Two-
Way Mirror*, and *I Can't Remember Anything* and *Clara*,
performed together as *Danger: Memory!*), Miller expanded *The
Last Yankee* from one brief scene between two husbands in
the waiting room to a longer one-act play that shifts the
focus to their wives in the hospital. In its final form, *The Last
Yankee*, technically a one-act play, continues Miller's long-
standing concern for the place of the worker in American
society, but this time adds to it the place of the patient on
the American stage.

   In 'About Theatre Language', an essay Miller appended
to an early edition of *The Last Yankee*, he explains that 'a
conventionally realistic work about mental illness would be

bound to drive to a reverberating climax. But repression is the cultural inheritance of these New Englanders and such theatricality would be a betrayal of *their* style of living and dying.' *The Last Yankee*, whose elements include the comic, the tragic and the absurd, shows how Miller continued remaking dramatic forms late in his career, new plays that once again emphasised the 'overtly stylized rather than "natural"'.

Miller called *The Last Yankee* a 'comedy about a tragedy'. The tragedy, in Miller's view, is more social than personal. Even as Patricia and Leroy recommit to their marriage, their ability to change the world around them is limited. In *The Last Yankee*, as in several of Miller's other later plays, especially *Broken Glass* and *Some Kind of Love Story*, the intimate nature of illness is more central to the drama than other kinds of personal or cultural crises. By using illness to critique America's 'success mythology', Miller focuses on how even seemingly powerless individuals might be able to take charge of their world. When Patricia rejects the help of so-called experts, she takes on their authority. The hospital's institutional space becomes a sanctuary where the patients, safe from meddling hands, become doctors themselves. On stage there are only female patients and their husbands, all of whom are seen as making decisions about when to come, when to leave and why. The first therapeutic relationship the audience sees within the hospital is between Karen and Patricia. Patricia, the more experienced patient, shows Karen how to work the system, how and why to keep the husbands waiting, when to take treatment and when to refuse it. Patricia's justification for taking over Karen's therapy is her apparent success in having commandeered her own: after three weeks of taking herself completely off medication, she feels better than ever. Unlike Karen, who is beginning to sense that her husband is the source of her illness, Patricia is beginning to see that her husband Leroy may be the source of her cure.

Even as Patricia and Karen have withdrawn from the domestic cultures they are expected to support, the hospital allows them to be supported instead. This reversal makes illness the vehicle by which the women leave home to go out and save themselves. That their salvation comes about in a taxpayer-funded, state-run mental institution, if it comes about at all, is crucial to Miller's upending of this stereotypically gendered world-view. At this hospital, Miller explains, 'there is a vast parking space because crowds of stricken citizens converge on this place to visit mothers, fathers, brothers, and sisters . . . the two patients we may be about to meet are not at all unique'. Note that Miller uses the term 'stricken' to refer not to the hospital's inmates but to those who visit them. By this definition, the families – here, the husbands – of those patients are the ones most in need of therapy. When Leroy admits at the end of the first act that 'for all I know I'm in line for this funny farm myself by now' (14), he shows the distance he has travelled. If the asylum is a theatre, he is ready for his turn upon the stage.

Characters

Leroy Hamilton
The last Yankee of the title, Leroy Hamilton is an accomplished carpenter who takes great pride in his work. Sitting in the waiting room with John Frick, a man whose former lumber business Leroy long patronised, he acts the part of a polite stranger. While Leroy initially confines his conversation to what he knows of the hospital routine, Frick's insecurity quickly draws him into a less superficial conversation about the illness both men's wives share. Leroy, more experienced in the role of the patient's spouse, can articulate better the toll Patricia's disease has taken on him. 'Start feeling sorry for yourself, that's when you're in trouble' (8), he says. Frick first mentions optimism, but that label belongs to Leroy; optimism defines him, making him the play's representative for what Miller believed was a core American value.

Leroy recoils from Frick when he feels attacked and patronised by the older, wealthier man. He resents being mistaken for someone supposedly better than a mere

carpenter, especially once Frick makes it clear no Hamilton
should have to work with his hands. Leroy's self-deprecation
as well as his manners break down in the face of Frick's
hypocrisy, as he finally demands 'what's it going to be,
equality or what kind of country?' (14). No part of this
argument revolves around the men's common concern, the
wives inside the hospital, although Leroy repeatedly uses
Patricia's hospitalisation to excuse his breach of good
manners. Instead, Leroy attempts to drive home the classic
Jeffersonian position on the dignity of labour, but to no
avail. At the end of the first scene, Frick still cannot
understand the slight he has offered and both men retreat to
the formalities of their initial positions.

Once inside the ward, when Leroy claims enjoyment of
the pleasures of the moment – skiing down a hill, playing
the banjo, using a good tool, breathing fresh air – he offers
Patricia a model for measuring success unconstrained by the
past or the future. Stating these ideas inside the hospital has
a salutary effect on Leroy, as he reclaims those values Frick
would have him abandon. Patricia reminds Leroy that his
family's expectations are even higher than hers, and that by
living a life devoted to avoiding their pressures, he has come
to be 'fifty times more depressed' than she is (31).

In the first scene, the audience sympathises with Leroy,
the well-meaning, overworked father of seven, especially so
when Frick inadvertently insults him. But by sharing her
diagnosis, Patricia defines a possibility for both herself and
her husband. Leroy has spent his life avoiding the burden of
his past, while Patricia has actively struggled with her own,
drugging herself into sleep when the struggle was too hard.
When Leroy eventually admits that he thinks her medical
problem is one of attitude, we see quite clearly that he has
been afraid to admit it is a problem they both share. Leroy
comes to realise that by working hard to avoid the kind of
success his own family expected of him, he has been as
obsessed with success as Patricia continues to be. He relies
on this measure for his judgement of human nature even as
he resents such judgements being made about himself. He
has defended himself against people like Frick for so long

that he has forgotten what Patricia soon reminds him of, that he is always really in competition with himself.

In the first scene with Leroy, Frick, by asserting the easy and customary privileges wealth has brought him, and then by failing to connect with his own wife in the second, gives Leroy an opportunity to see himself in a new light. By articulating with monstrous clarity the assumptions of class and privilege that Leroy feels obliged to reject, Frick forces Leroy to the point where he can acknowledge that as much as he has been right about the causes of Patricia's illness, she is also right about him. 'Well, all I hope is that I'm the last Yankee,' he says, 'so people can start living today instead of a hundred years ago' (34). When Patricia, drug-free, agrees to leave the hospital with him, Leroy regains the equilibrium and dignity Frick tried to take away from him.

John Frick

John Frick, in many ways, brings together many personal characteristics Miller found distasteful. A wealthy man, or at least a big fish in a small pond, Frick exudes both thoughtlessness and privilege. From his first appearance in Scene One, he conveys his impatience with events he cannot control, and discomfort in spaces where his social status buys him no favours. His clipped language in the opening conversation suggests a man unaccustomed to explaining himself, or making excuses for his assumptions, even racist ones. Miller stacks the deck against Frick early in the play, making it all the more interesting when Frick eventually becomes the object of more sympathy than scorn.

Frick serves an important expository role in the first scene. As the relative newcomer, he asks the questions the audience needs to know about the play's setting and characters – who, where, why, when – forcing Leroy to share his knowledge and explain his own role in the drama. When it comes to the hospital and its rituals, Frick, like his wife inside, performs as a novice while the more experienced Hamiltons teach both Fricks the ropes. In the first scene Frick attempts to make Leroy over in his own image, as though no comfort, or even accurate information, can come from someone Frick sees as fundamentally different from himself. Because it does not occur to Frick to question his own social role, he struggles to see himself as Leroy sees him. Where Leroy identifies himself by the things he does, Frick's self-image comes from what he owns: a lumberyard, an oil business, a car dealership. He misses the days when Karen, too, valued what they owned, 'real estate, stock market, always interested' her he claims, until one day, they did not. In the middle of the first scene, when he begins to notice who Leroy really is, Frick remains so deeply attached to his own unexamined values that he cannot see why Leroy would find his assumptions suspect and offensive. In Frick's world, being mistaken for a banker (or a contractor, in any event, 'a college man') can only be seen as a compliment.

Just as Leroy Hamilton squirms under the weight of his famous ancestor, Miller uses Frick's name to make his character stand for ruthless capitalism and the power of the system over the individual. When Frick states his admiration for Alexander Hamilton, he casts in his lot with an industrial, autocratic vision of America, one Henry Clay Frick both venerated and represented. Leroy, on the other hand, identifies with the workers, especially those skilled artisans resisting the efforts of industry to make them mere cogs in the machine. Even when Frick must rely on workers like Leroy, whether to buy his timber or mend his showerhead, he resents their demands to be treated as equals, to be respected as equally productive members of society. At the same time, Frick, a wealthy man who appreciates fine things, recognises Leroy's skill at carpentry, praising his work for the Presbyterian church. Frick embodies a contradiction: he can afford to take Karen to the Rogers Pavilion, but refuses to do so; he admires the products of Leroy's labour, but resents what he considers a working man's overly generous wages; obviously pained by his wife's condition, he can, however, only speak about the way it affects his life rather than hers.

When Frick returns to the stage near the end of the

second scene, he becomes somewhat less high-handed than when he told Leroy that he obviously had not studied enough in school. Now that the suitcase he carried in the first scene is revealed to contain Karen's tap costume, some of his pretension drops away. While Karen changes, Frick expresses his gratitude to Patricia, amazed at how her advice has helped reanimate his wife. The ease with which Frick thanks Patricia, rather than assumes that Karen's doctors and their therapies have improved her mood, shows the distance he has travelled since the play began.

Patricia Hamilton

Patricia Hamilton, the play's most articulate figure, lives at the intersection of several different perspectives, each of which offers an alternative explanation for her condition and her life. The doctors she sees treat her for clinical depression, her husband Leroy thinks that she is disappointed in life because her family's unnaturally high expectations for her conflicted with reality, and her minister perceives her to be 'in a constant state of prayer' (18). Patricia's trajectory in the play depends upon which of these competing viewpoints, if any, she chooses to own. Even though she remains in the hospital, she dismisses the physicians' diagnosis just as she has rejected their medications. Only she can decide when it is time for her to leave.

The audience first sees Patricia chasing a ping-pong ball across the stage. She soon leads Karen Frick away from the game – 'Come let's talk . . . I hate these games' (16) – and comments that the other patients are too depressed to exercise. These words and actions contrast markedly with Leroy's earlier description of Patricia as fearful, withdrawn and agoraphobic. Despite her energy and apparent focus, Patricia seems unmoored from her current life, talking more about her long-dead brothers than about any of her seven children, all of whom live at home. *The Last Yankee* takes place seven weeks into Patricia's third hospitalisation within a period of two years. Patricia, who stopped taking

medication three weeks ago, tells Karen 'it's the longest I've
been clean in almost fifteen years' (17). Compared to the
Fricks, she and Leroy seem to understand the dynamics of
clinical depression, yet this time Patricia's withdrawal from
family life is driving Leroy to breaking-point.

Just as Leroy's Hamiltonian origins define much of his
character, Patricia is formed by her immigrant Swedish
family and their complex history. In this context, the
Yankees were the establishment while the Swedes were
unwelcome newcomers. Frick may see Leroy's carpentry as
evidence of a fine family's decline, but Patricia has been
paralysed by her family's rise in the social and economic
sphere. Little wonder she surmises that her husband is the
one who is depressed. Compared with the Yankee
establishment represented in the play by the Hamiltons, the
Sorgensons are relative newcomers in New England, part of
a wave of nineteenth-century immigrants from Northern
Europe. Patricia describes the Swedes' rough landing in
America, where 'some Yankee doctors wouldn't come out to
a Swedish home to deliver a baby' (34) and Swedes were
exploited by their neighbours as cheap labour. Ironically, it
appears that the play's families have switched places:
Patricia's siblings are the ones who want her treated in the
expensive, private Rogers Pavilion, 'saying it's a disgrace for
their sister to be in a public institution', while Leroy prefers
the state hospital because, after all, 'I'm the public!' (9).
Patricia has become a patrician in her own mind, and sees
depression as a legitimate response to the sad economic facts
governing her marriage and life.

Early in Scene Two, Patricia seems attracted to the
spiritual alternatives, echoing the religious language of her
Lutheran upbringing and the Baptist minister she has lately
been visiting. Perhaps because she is in hospital, religious
alternatives tempt her now more than ever. 'The soul
belongs to God' (19), she piously declares. But Patricia casts
her spiritual journey in secular terms, as if she is never fully
removed from more earthbound desires. 'This minister I
mentioned?' she tells Karen . . . 'when he left his previous
church they gave him a Pontiac Grand Am' (18). Talking to

Karen, she begins to acknowledge her illness's roots in her attitude toward Leroy, although she still couches this revelation in religious terms. 'It came to me like a visitation,' she tells Karen, and 'I lost all desire for medication' (20).

Leroy has always thought her recovery lay in a life of simple pleasures centred in the here and now, not in the past or future. In the confines of the hospital, and away from church and off drugs, Patricia begins to see the value of Leroy's dogged determination even as she continues to fear succumbing to it. Leroy's steadfastness becomes Patricia's salvation. As much as she reveres her dynamic and accomplished brothers, she knows that two of them were victims of the same psychological disorder afflicting her.

The Last Yankee ends when Patricia makes her decision to leave the hospital and embrace her life as it is. Karen's dance routine gives Patricia and Leroy a chance to cooperate, to work together to help someone even more troubled than they are. Karen, by virtue of her money and social position, disproves what Patricia hopes and Leroy fears – that money equals happiness. From Karen's experience, Patricia learns that a supportive husband who drives an old car might in fact be a much better partner than any wealth might bring.

Karen Frick

Karen Frick elicits the most pathos among *The Last Yankee*'s quartet. In her sixties, she is a generation older than Patricia Hamilton, yet she seems much more childlike in her timidity and dependency on others' opinions. John Frick tells Leroy that Karen has only been in hospital for a few days, and he cannot fathom what Karen could possibly be disturbed about. 'I don't care what happens to the country,' he says, 'there's nothing could ever hurt her any more. Suddenly, out of nowhere, she's terrified!' (8). Unlike her husband, who is uncomfortable even with the hospital's black staff, Karen fears what is already inside her own home.

When the audience firsts meets her, her actions convey

anxiety and unease. She seems unsure of what to do, relying on Patricia to tell her to 'sit down' and 'relax', as if she would otherwise have stayed in her awkward position for the remainder of the scene (17). Recently hospitalised, Karen is on medication that exacerbates any inherent level of shyness; Patricia mentions pills twice, advising her, 'whatever they tell you, you have to cut down the medication' (21). One symptom of her confusion is her inability or unwillingness to follow Patricia's conversational lead. Karen's speech is full of *non sequiturs*, and she appears not to notice Patricia's efforts to shift the conversation on to another ground. But her musings are not as random as they may first appear to be. Karen sounds distracted because Patricia barely allows her to speak. String together Karen's early attempts to talk to Patricia, however, and a story appears about the overdose of pills that has led to her confinement.

Ironically, Karen later admits to feeling ashamed because Patricia has so many thoughts; Karen does not feel she has enough. In reality, Karen thinks a great deal; however, it has been a long time since anyone else has paid any attention to them. Frick provides everything he thinks his wife could desire, but it is not until Patricia tells him that he must 'be careful not to sound so disappointed in her' (41) that he even realises that his attitude towards his wife might have some bearing on her unenviable situation. Towards the end of the second scene, Karen perks up enough to share her one passion with her new friend. At Karen's request, Frick has brought her tap-dancing costume to the hospital and, as she unpacks her shorts, shoes and top hat, Karen asks him to sing 'Swanee River' so that she can dance for her friend. Under pressure, Frick obliges for a moment, but is intensely embarrassed by his wife's display. What is the audience to make of this woman in her sixties tap-dancing in the hospital? Accompanied by her husband's singing, the stage directions indicate that she '*dances a bit more boldly, a joyous freedom starting into her*' (44). Once she progresses from '*freedom*' to '*a hint of the sensuous*', Frick cannot stand to watch the spectacle any longer, even as he participates in it.

From one perspective, Karen's dance looks like Nora's *tarantella* in Ibsen's *A Doll's House* – a woman, otherwise confined in a domestic role, dancing in a wild, liberated fashion in front of her husband. As Karen approaches '*freedom*', her husband loses what is left of the self-control he values so highly. If the traditional celebratory nature of the dance symbolises happy endings, social order and matrimony, then a dancing wife whose performance is disrupted by a furious husband indicates chaos, perhaps even abandonment.

Yet at the same time as the dancer demonstrates freedom from bondage, she is also separated from reason. Karen's dance, while unsettling, might also be interpreted as a harmless, therapeutic pursuit, perhaps even recuperative. But to Frick it is not at all charming, and it is not harmless. He sees his timid, agoraphobic wife suddenly transformed into an extroverted and sexualised performer, who has emerged from her secret basement studio to display herself before anyone who can be persuaded to watch. Patricia, trying to encourage Karen, keeps telling Frick to 'look at' his wife as he finally explodes, 'I am looking at her, goddammit! (*This astonishing furious shout, his reddened face, stops everything. A look of fear is on* **Karen***'s face*)' (44). For a moment he tries to compose himself with rigidity and restraint, and tells Karen that 'it don't mean I'm disappointed, dear'; but he can see no choice other than to walk out. Karen is clearly devastated by his outburst, as if physically stricken. The stage directions indicate that '*She keeps staring at him . . . He abruptly turns and exits . . .* **Karen** *stands perfectly still, staring at nothing*' (45). When Frick walks off the stage, their intimacy, like her illness, remains in perilous limbo.

The play in performance

The Last Yankee first appeared on stage in June 1991, as part of the Marathon Annual Festival of One-Act Plays at New York's Ensemble Studio Theatre. Although *The Last Yankee*'s final version is itself a one-act play in two scenes, only the first scene between Leroy and Frick was performed in the festival. In 1993 *The Last Yankee* had a dual premiere, opening in New York on 21 January and in London on 26 January. The New York production, directed by John Tillinger, played at the Manhattan Theatre Club, starring John Heard as Leroy Hamilton, Tom Aldredge as John Frick, Frances Conroy as Patricia Hamilton and Rose Gregario as Karen Frick. Charlotte Meier played the unnamed Patient. In London, David Healy (Frick), Peter Davison (Leroy), Zoë Wanamaker (Patricia), and Helen Burns (Karen), with Bethany Hanson playing the unnamed Patient, appeared under the direction of David Thacker at the Young Vic. On 20 April, the production transferred to the Duke of York's Theatre in the West End, with Margot Leicester in the role of Patricia. In New York, as in London, the cast and directors were greatly admired, though the play itself opened to mixed reviews. Theatre reviews for the twin premieres of *The Last Yankee* bring up many of the same points: wonder at Miller's late-in-life productivity, disappointment at the short form of the one-act play, admiration for the character of Leroy and, to a lesser extent, for Patricia, though critics were confused by Miller's portrayal of the Fricks.

In the *Wall Street Journal*, Melanie Kirkpatrick wrote, 'Arthur Miller is not dead . . . the fact is that not a lot has been heard from him in recent years – at least not in this country.' She went on to praise the play and its production, calling it 'the work of a master craftsman and . . . testament to Mr. Miller's genius at elevating ordinary events into poetry'. Howard Kissel, in the *Daily News*, praised the New York cast, particularly Frances Conroy, whom he found 'especially moving as the carpenter's wife, veering nervously between newfound security and doubt, giving her final confidence an after-battle glow'.

In London, David Thacker's direction, Shelagh Keegan's minimalist, translucent set and the play itself all came in for high praise. Malcolm Rutherford, writing in the *Financial Times*, called Karen Frick's tap dance 'one of the most moving scenes I have ever seen in a modern play . . . her humanity is overwhelming'. Ian Shuttleworth, in *City Limits*, said 'Peter Davison's Leroy keeps the character's faults welcomely to the fore to dispel notions of saintliness, and Zoë Wanamaker as [Patricia] movingly depicts a depressive's struggle to attain the ordinary. The final moments, in which Mrs Frick tapdances in top hat and shorts to her husband's stunted rendition of "Swanee River", is the very antithesis of the saccharin so many lesser writers would make of it.'

In 1998 *The Last Yankee* was revived at the Signature Theatre in New York, under the direction of the legendary Joseph Chaikin, as part of an Arthur Miller season. This time *The Last Yankee* filled half the bill, being paired with the shorter Miller one-act *I Can't Remember Anything*. The double-bill format made *The Last Yankee* look more substantial by comparison with the shorter *I Can't Remember Anything*, and the pairing served to emphasise the intended chamber scale of *The Last Yankee*. Writing in the *New York Times*, Ben Brantley noted the play's 'deliberately circular and repetitive' structure, using 'ordinary domestic exchanges to explore the big themes that have always been dear to the playwright's heart: the blight of the American myth of success, the crippling powers of memory, and the struggle to continue through a life that seems devoid of meaning'. Since that revival, the play has entered the repertory of numerous theatres in the UK, the United States and Austria.

Revisions

The first edition of *The Last Yankee* shows some notable differences to the present one. This is not unusual in Miller's work since he frequently made minor changes to his scripts, for instance changing monetary figures to keep up with inflation or the name of a disease to reflect a more current cultural awareness. Other changes affect stage directions, which might have an impact on readers and actors in different ways.

In the first American edition, Leroy, as well as Frick's
plumber, earned seventeen dollars an hour. In the first
British edition, published the following year, Miller raised
their rate from seventeen to twenty-seven dollars an hour.
As time goes on, even the higher figure seems inadequate
for a skilled tradesman. More important, however, is how
the play contextualises the amount in question. If Frick and
Leroy establish the value of the figure through their
conversation, discrepancies between the figure they name
and going rates for trade work become less important. In
the future, the figure will seem even smaller, but as the play
becomes less contemporary, audiences will perhaps ignore
the difference. This edition retains the original wage.

A second revision concerns Patricia and Karen's
medication. In the earlier, American version, Patricia tells
Karen 'the soul belongs to God, we're not supposed to be
stuffing Valium into His mouth'. Miller later changed
Valium to Prozac. Valium, a benzodiazepine frequently
prescribed for anxiety, was first approved for use in the
United States in 1960, and was among the most widely
prescribed prescription drugs in America during much of
the 1960s and 1970s. In the context of *The Last Yankee*,
however, the name Valium presents one specific problem –
given its sedative properties, it is one of the last drugs a
doctor would prescribe for depression. Prozac, on the other
hand, was as well known as Valium by the time of the play's
premieres and, while still controversial, is indicated
specifically for depression. Both drugs have been depicted in
popular culture as pills that make everything better or,
alternatively, drugs frequently abused by those seeking a
quick fix for real problems, but Prozac is a better fit for
Miller's theme.

The most significant change concerns a character whom
readers frequently ignore but whose presence on stage can
matter a great deal: the unnamed Patient. All previous
editions feature the Patient in the cast list and in the stage
direction that opens Scene Two, Miller notes '*she will not
move throughout the scene*'. At the play's end, however, the stage
directions in the American and British editions are markedly

different. The American version's final stage direction reads, '*The woman on the bed stirs, then falls back and remains motionless. A stillness envelops the whole stage*', while in the British edition Miller changed the direction to end with '*The patient on the bed remains motionless. A stillness envelops the whole stage, immobility seems eternal.*' There are several issues at play here. One, purely practical, is that an entirely immobile Patient need not necessarily be played by a living (i.e. paid) actor when a mannequin might suffice. On a more interpretive level, however, a Patient who shows no sign of life may communicate a substantively different message to the audience from one who moves and then falls still. Given that the Patient has slept through the whole second scene, including Karen's tap dance and Leroy's banjo playing, audiences might reasonably assume that she has been medicated into unconsciousness. Earlier stage directions, consistent through all editions, also suggest that the unnamed Patient is Patricia's roommate. However, Patricia herself never seems to notice the woman at all, either to comment on her comatose state, or to express caution or care that she might be bothered by any amount of talk or action. This suggests that the unnamed Patient exists only for the final tableau, and Miller's final choice suggests that to be left in the hospital – Karen's fate – is to risk being mistaken for dead. This edition reinstates the final stage direction from the play's first American edition.

Further Reading

Works by Miller

Arthur Miller Plays, 6 vols with introductions by Miller (vol. 1: *All My Sons, Death of a Salesman, The Crucible, A Memory of Two Mondays, A View from the Bridge*; vol. 2: *The Misfits, After the Fall, Incident at Vichy, The Price, Creation of the World, Playing for Time*; vol. 3: *The American Clock, The Archbishop's Ceiling, Two-Way Mirror*; vol. 4: *The Golden Years, The Man Who Had All the Luck, I Can't Remember Anything, Clara*; vol. 5: *The Last Yankee, The Ride Down Mount Morgan, Almost Everybody Wins*; vol. 6: *Broken Glass, Mr Peter's Connections, Resurrection Blues, Finishing the Picture*). London: Methuen Drama, 1988–2009

After the Fall, with commentary and notes by Brenda Murphy. London: Methuen Drama, 2011

All My Sons, with commentary and notes by Toby Zinman. London: Methuen Drama, 2010

The Crucible, with commentary and notes by Susan C.W. Abbotson. London: Methuen Drama, 2010

Death of a Salesman, with commentary and notes by Enoch Brater. London: Methuen Drama, 2010

A Memory of Two Mondays, with commentary and notes by Joshua Polster. London: Methuen Drama, 2011

The Price, with commentary and notes by Jane K. Dominik. London: Methuen Drama, 2011

A View from the Bridge, with commentary and notes by Stephen Marino. London: Methuen Drama, 2010

The Portable Arthur Miller, ed. Christopher Bigsby. New York: Penguin, 2003

'About Theatre Language', Introduction to *Miller Plays: 5*. London: Methuen Drama, 2009

Echoes Down the Corridor: Collected Essays 1944–2000, ed. Steven R. Centola. London: Methuen, 2000

The Theatre Essays of Arthur Miller, ed. Robert A. Martin. London:
  Methuen, 1994
Timebends: A Life. London: Methuen, 1987

Interviews with Miller

Balakian, Janet, 'An Interview with Arthur Miller'. *Studies in
  American Drama, 1945–Present*, 6.1 (1991), 29–47
Bigsby, Christopher, ed., *Arthur Miller and Company: Arthur Miller
  Talks About His Work in the Company of Actors, Designers, Directors,
  Reviewers and Writers*. London: Methuen, 1990
Brater, Enoch, 'A Conversation with Arthur Miller', in *Arthur
  Miller's America: Theater and Culture in a Time of Change*, ed.
  Enoch Brater. Ann Arbor: University of Michigan Press,
  244–55
Centola, Steven R., 'The Last Yankee: An Interview with Arthur
  Miller'. *American Drama*, 5.1 (1995), 78–98
Gussow, Mel, *Conversations with Miller*. New York: Applause, 2002
Roudané, Matthew C., ed., *Conversations with Arthur Miller*.
  Jackson: University Press of Mississippi, 1987

Biographical studies of Miller

Bigsby, Christopher, *Arthur Miller 1915–1962*. London:
  Weidenfeld & Nicolson, 2008
Brater, Enoch, *Arthur Miller: A Playwright's Life and Works*. London:
  Thames & Hudson, 2005
Gottfried, Martin, *Arthur Miller: His Life and Work*. Cambridge,
  MA: Da Capo Press, 2003

Critical approaches to Miller

Abbotson, Susan C.W., *Critical Companion to Arthur Miller: A
  Literary Reference to His Life and Work*. New York: Facts on File,
  2007
Bigsby, Christopher, ed., *The Cambridge Companion to Arthur Miller*.
  Cambridge: Cambridge University Press, 1997

Bigsby, Christopher, *Arthur Miller: A Critical Study*. Cambridge: Cambridge University Press, 2005

Brater, Enoch, *Arthur Miller's America: Theater and Culture in a Time of Change*. Ann Arbor: University of Michigan Press, 2005

Brater, Enoch, ed., *Arthur Miller's Global Theater: How an American Playwright Is Performed on Stages Around the World*. Ann Arbor: University of Michigan Press, 2007

Otten, Terry, *The Temptation of Innocence in the Dramas of Arthur Miller*. Columbia, MO: University of Missouri Press, 2002

Shorter studies of *The Last Yankee*

Abbotson, Susan C.W., 'Reconnecting and Reasserting the Self: The Art of Compromise in Arthur Miller's *The Last Yankee*'. *South Atlantic Review*, 63.4 (1998), 58–76

Osterwalder, Hans, 'Madness in the Family in Realistic and Absurd Guise: Miller's *The Last Yankee* and Pinter's *Moonlight*'. *Studia Anglica Posnaniensia*, 34 (1999), 319–31

Scanlan, Robert, 'The Late Plays of Arthur Miller', in *Arthur Miller's America: Theatre and Culture in a Time of Change*, ed. Enoch Brater. Ann Arbor: University of Michigan Press, 180–90

Smith, William, 'Damn Yankee! Leroy Hamilton Crafts Wood With Passion and Honesty, But Who in Modern America Cares?' in *Miller and Middle America: Essays on Arthur Miller and the American Experience*, ed. Paula T. Langteau. Lanham, MD: University Press of America, 2007, 89–97

Tai, Stephan, 'Arthur Miller's *Last Yankee* – A Male Depressive'. *Contemporary Review*, March (1994), 147–8

The Last Yankee

Characters

Frick
Leroy
Patricia
Karen
Patient

Scene One

The visiting room of a state mental hospital. **Leroy Hamilton** *is seated on one of the half-dozen chairs idly leafing through an old magazine. He is forty-eight, trim, dressed in subdued Ivy League jacket and slacks and shined brogues. A banjo case rests against his chair.*

Mr Frick *enters. He is sixty, solid, in a business suit. He carries a small valise. He looks about, glances at* **Leroy**, *just barely nods, and sits ten feet away. He looks at his watch, then impatiently at the room.* **Leroy** *goes on leafing through the magazine.*

Frick (*pointing right*) 'Supposed to notify somebody in there?

Leroy (*indicating left*) Did you give your name to the attendant?

Frick Yes. 'Seem to be paying much attention, though.

Leroy 'They know you're here, then. He calls through to the ward.

Returns to his magazine.

Frick (*slight pause*) Tremendous parking space down there. They need that for?

Leroy Well a lot of people visit on weekends. Fills up pretty much.

Frick Really? That whole area?

Leroy Pretty much.

Frick 'Doubt that.

He goes to the window and looks out. Pause.

Beautifully landscaped, got to say that for it.

Leroy Yes, it's a very nice place.

Frick 'See them walking around out there it's hard to tell. 'Stopped one to ask directions and only realized when he stuck out his finger and pointed at my nose.

Leroy Heh-heh.

Frick   Quite a shock. Sitting there reading some thick book and crazy as a coot. You'd never know.

He sits in another chair. **Leroy** *returns to the magazine. He studies* **Leroy**.

Frick   Is it your wife?

Leroy   Yes.

Frick   I've got mine in there too.

Leroy   Uh, huh.

He stares ahead, politely refraining from the magazine.

Frick   My name's Frick.

Leroy   Hi. I'm Hamilton.

Frick   Gladameetu.

Slight pause.

How do you find it here?

Leroy   I guess they do a good job.

Frick   Surprisingly well-kept for a state institution.

Leroy   Oh, ya.

Frick   Awful lot of colored, though, ain't there?

Leroy   Quite a few, ya.

Frick   Yours been in long?

Leroy   Going on seven weeks now.

Frick   They give you any idea when she can get out?

Leroy   Oh, I could take her out now, but I won't for a couple weeks.

Frick   Why's that?

Leroy   Well this is her third time.

Frick   'Don't say.

Leroy   I'd like them to be a little more sure before I take her out again . . . Although you can never *be* sure.

Frick   That fairly common? – that they have to come back?

Leroy   About a third they say. This your first time, I guess.

Frick   I just brought her in last Tuesday. I certainly hope she doesn't have to stay long. They ever say what's wrong with her?

Leroy   She's a depressive.

Frick   Really. That's what they say about mine. Just gets . . . sort of sad?

Leroy   It's more like . . . frightened.

Frick   Sounds just like mine. Got so she wouldn't even leave the house.

Leroy   That's right.

Frick   Oh, yours too?

Leroy   Ya, she wouldn't go out. Not if she could help it, anyway.

Frick   She ever hear sounds?

Leroy   She used to. Like a loud humming.

Frick   Same thing! Ts. What do you know! – How old is she?

Leroy   She's forty-four.

Frick   Is that all! I had an idea it had something to do with getting old . . .

Leroy   I don't think so. My wife is still – I wouldn't say a raving beauty, but she's still . . . a pretty winsome woman. They're usually sick a long time before you realize it, you know. I just never realized it.

Frick   Mine never showed any signs at all. Just a nice, quiet kind of a woman. Always slept well . . .

Leroy   Well mine sleeps well too.

Frick Really?

Leroy Lots of them love to sleep. I found that out. She'd take naps every afternoon. Longer and longer.

Frick Mine too. But then about six, eight months ago she got nervous about keeping the doors locked. And then the windows. I had to air condition the whole house. I finally had to do the shopping, she just wouldn't go out.

Leroy Oh, I've done the shopping for twenty years.

Frick You don't say!

Leroy Well, you just never think of it as a sickness. I like to ski, for instance, or ice-skating . . . she'd never come along. Or swimming in the summer. I always took the kids alone . . .

Frick Oh you have children.

Leroy Yes. Seven.

Frick Seven! – I've been wondering if it was because she never had any.

Leroy No, that's not it. – You don't have *any*?

Frick No. We kept putting it off, and then it got too late, and first thing you know . . . it's just too late.

Leroy For a while there I thought maybe she had too *many* children . . .

Frick Well I don't have any, so . . .

Leroy Yeah, I guess that's not it either.

Slight pause.

Frick I just can't figure it out. There's no bills; we're very well fixed; she's got a beautiful home . . . There's really not a trouble in the world. Although, God knows, maybe that's the trouble . . .

Leroy Oh no, I got plenty of bills and it didn't help mine. I don't think it's how many bills you have.

Frick   What do you think it is, then?

Leroy   Don't ask me, I don't know.

Frick   When she started locking up everything I thought maybe it's these Negroes, you know? There's an awful lot of fear around; all this crime.

Leroy   I don't think. so. My wife was afraid before there were any Negroes. I mean, around.

Frick   Well, one thing came out of it – I finally learned how to make coffee. And mine's better than hers was. It's an awful sensation, though – coming home and there's nobody there.

Leroy   How'd you like to come home and there's seven of them there?

Frick   I guess I'm lucky at that.

Leroy   Well, I am too. They're wonderful kids.

Frick   They still very young?

Leroy   Five to nineteen. But they all pitch in. Everything's clean, house runs like a ship.

Frick   You're lucky to have good children these days. – I guess we're both lucky.

Leroy   That's the only way to look at it. Start feeling sorry for yourself, that's when you're in trouble.

Frick   Awfully hard to avoid sometimes.

Leroy   You can't give in to it though. Like today – I was so disgusted I just laid down and . . . I was ready to throw in the chips. But then I got up and washed my face, put on the clothes, and here I am. After all, she can't help it either, who are you going to blame?

Frick   It's a mystery – a woman with everything she could possibly want. I don't care what happens to the country, there's nothing could ever hurt her any more. Suddenly, out of nowhere, she's terrified! . . . She lost all her optimism. Yours do that? Lose her optimism?

Leroy   Mine was never very optimistic. She's Swedish.

Frick   Oh. Mine certainly was. Whatever deal I was in, couldn't wait till I got home to talk about it. Real estate, stock market, always interested. All of a sudden, no interest whatsoever. Might as well be talking to that wall over there. – Your wife have brothers and sisters?

Leroy   Quite a few, ya.

Frick   Really. I even thought maybe it's that she was an only child, and if she had brothers and sisters to talk to . . .

Leroy   Oh no – at least I don't think so. It could be even worse.

Frick   They don't help, huh?

Leroy   They *think* they're helping. Come around saying it's a disgrace for their sister to be in a public institution. That's the kind of help. So I said, 'Well, I'm the public!'

Frick   Sure! – It's a perfectly nice place.

Leroy   They want her in the Rogers Pavilion.

Frick   Rogers! – That's a couple of hundred dollars a day minimum . . .

Leroy   Well if I had that kind of money I wouldn't mind, but . . .

Frick   No-no, don't you do it. I could afford it, but what are we paying taxes for?

Leroy   So they can go around saying their sister's in the Rogers Pavilion, that's all.

Frick   Out of the question. That's fifty thousand dollars a year. Plus tips. I'm sure you have to tip them there.

Leroy   Besides, it's eighty miles there and back, I could never get to see her . . .

Frick   If they're so sensitive you ought to tell *them* to pay for it. That'd shut them up, I bet.

Leroy   Well no – they've offered to pay part. Most of it, in fact.

Frick   Whyn't you do it, then?

Leroy (*holding a secret*)   I didn't think it's a good place for her.

Frick   Why? – if they'd pay for it? It's one of the top places in the country. Some very rich people go there.

Leroy   I know.

Frick   And the top doctors, you know. And they order whatever they want to eat. I went up there to look it over; no question about it, it's absolutely first class, much better than this place. You should take them up on it.

Leroy   I'd rather have her here.

Frick   Well I admire your attitude. You don't see that kind of pride any more.

Leroy   It's not pride, exactly.

Frick   Never mind, it's a great thing, keep it up. Everybody's got the gimmes, it's destroying the country. Had a man in a few weeks ago to put in a new shower-head. Nothing to it. Screw off the old one and screw on the new one. Seventeen dollars an hour!

Leroy   Yeah, well.

Gets up, unable to remain seated.

Everybody's got to live, I guess.

Frick   I take my hat off to you – that kind of independence. Don't happen to be with Colonial Trust, do you?

Leroy   No.

Frick   There was something familiar about you. What line are you in?

Leroy (*he is at the window now, staring out. Slight pause*)   Carpenter.

Frick (*taken aback*)   Don't say . . . Contractor?

Leroy   No. Just carpenter. – I take on one or two fellas when I have to, but I work alone most of the time.

Frick   I'd never have guessed it.

Leroy   Well that's what I do.

Looks at his watch, wanting escape.

Frick   I mean your whole . . . your way of dressing and everything.

Leroy   Why? Just ordinary clothes.

Frick   No, you look like a college man.

Leroy   Most of them have long hair, don't they?

Frick   The way college men used to look. I've spent thirty years around carpenters, that's why it surprised me. You know Frick Supply, don't you?

Leroy   Oh ya. I've bought quite a lot of wood from Frick.

Frick   I sold out about five years ago . . .

Leroy   I know. I used to see you around there.

Frick   You did? Why didn't you mention it?

Leroy (*shrugs*)   Just didn't.

Frick   You say Anthony?

Leroy   No, Hamilton. Leroy.

Frick (*points at him*)   Hey now! Of course! There was a big article about you in the *Herald* a couple of years ago. Descended from Alexander Hamilton.

Leroy   That's right.

Frick   Sure! No wonder! (*Holding out his palm as to a photo.*) Now that I visualize you in overalls, I think I recognize you. In fact, you were out in the yard loading plywood the morning that article came out. My bookkeeper pointed you out through the window. It's those clothes – if I'd seen you in overalls I'd've recognized you right off. Well, what do you know? (*The air of* *condescension plus wonder.*) Amazing thing what clothes'll do, isn't it. – Keeping busy?

Leroy   I get work.

Frick   What are you fellas charging now?

Leroy   I get seventeen an hour.

Frick   Good for you.

Leroy   I hate asking that much but even so I just about make it.

Frick   Shouldn't feel that way; if they'll pay it, grab it.

Leroy   Well ya, but it's still a lot of money. – My head's still back there thirty years ago.

Frick   What are you working on now?

Leroy   I'm renovating a colonial near Waverly. I just finished over in Belleville. The Presbyterian Church.

Frick   Did you do *that*?

Leroy   Yeah, just finished Wednesday.

Frick   That's a beautiful job. You're a good man. Where'd they get that altar?

Leroy   I built that.

Frick   That altar?

Leroy   Uh huh.

Frick   Hell, that's first-class! Huh! You must be doing all right.

Leroy   Just keeping ahead of it.

Frick (*slight pause*)   How'd it happen?

Leroy   What's that?

Frick   Well, coming out of an old family like that – how do you come to being a carpenter?

Leroy   Just . . . liked it.

Frick   Father a carpenter?

Leroy   No.

Frick   What was your father?

Leroy   Lawyer.

Frick   Why didn't you?

Leroy   Just too dumb, I guess.

Frick   Couldn't buckle down to the books, huh?

Leroy   I guess not.

Frick   Your father should've taken you in hand.

Leroy (*sits with magazine, opening it*)   He didn't like the law either.

Frick   Even so. – Many of the family still around?

Leroy   Well, my mother, and two brothers.

Frick   No, I mean of the Hamiltons.

Leroy   Well they're Hamiltons.

Frick   I know, but I mean – some of them must be pretty important people.

Leroy   I wouldn't know. I never kept track of them.

Frick   You should. Probably some of them must be pretty big. – Never even looked them up?

Leroy   Nope.

Frick (*slight pause*)   You realize the importance of Alexander Hamilton, don't you?

Leroy   I know about him, more or less.

Frick   More or less! He was one of the most important Founding Fathers.

Leroy   I guess so, ya.

Frick   You read about him, didn't you?

Leroy   Well sure . . . I read about him.

Frick   Well didn't your father talk about him?

Leroy   Some. But he didn't care for him much.

Frick   Didn't care for *Alexander Hamilton*?

Leroy   It was something to do with his philosophy. But I never kept up with the whole thing.

Frick (*laughing, shaking his head*)   Boy, you're quite a character, aren't you.

Leroy *is silent, reddening.* **Frick** *continues chuckling at him for a moment.*

Leroy   I hope to God your wife is cured, Mr Frick, I hope she never has to come back here again.

Frick (*sensing the hostility*)   What have I said?

Leroy   This is the third time in two years for mine, and I don't mean to be argumentative but it's got me right at the end of my rope. For all I know I'm in line for this funny farm myself by now, but I have to tell you that this could be what's driving so many people crazy.

Frick   What is?

Leroy   This.

Frick   This what?

Leroy   This whole kind of conversation.

Frick   Why? What's wrong with it?

Leroy   Well never mind.

Frick   I don't know what you're talking about.

Leroy   Well what's it going to be, equality or what kind of country? – I mean am I supposed to be ashamed I'm a carpenter?

Frick   Who said you . . . ?

Leroy Then why do you talk like this to a man? One minute my altar is terrific and the next minute I'm some kind of shit bucket.

Frick Hey now, wait a minute . . .

Leroy I don't mean anything against you personally, I know you're a successful man and more power to you, but this whole type of conversation about my clothes – should I be ashamed I'm a carpenter? I mean everybody's talking 'labor, labor,' how much labor's getting; well if it's so great to be labor how come nobody wants to be it? I mean you ever hear a parent going around saying (*Mimes thumb pridefully tucked into suspenders.*) 'My son is a carpenter?' Do you? Do you ever hear people brag about a bricklayer? I don't know what you are but I'm only a dumb swamp Yankee, but . . . (*Suddenly breaks off with a shameful laugh.*) Excuse me. I'm really sorry. But you come back here two-three more times and you're liable to start talking the way you were never brought up to. (*Opens magazine.*)

Frick I don't understand what you're so hot about.

Leroy (*looks up from the magazine. Seems to start to explain, then sighs*) Nothing.

He returns to his magazine. **Frick** *shakes his head with a certain condescension, then goes back to the window, and looks out.*

Frick It's one hell of a parking lot, you have to say that for it.

They sit down for a long moment in silence, each in his own thoughts.

Blackout

Scene Two

Most of the stage is occupied by **Patricia**'s *bedroom. In one of the beds a fully clothed* **Patient** *lies motionless with one arm over her eyes. She will not move throughout the scene.*

Outside this bedroom is a corner of the Recreation Room, bare but for a few scattered chairs.

*Presently . . . from just offstage the sound of a Ping-Pong game. The ball comes bouncing into the Recreation Room area and **Patricia Hamilton** enters chasing it. She captures it and with a sigh of boredom goes offstage with it. The **Patient** is oblivious.*

We hear two or three pings and the ball comes onstage again with **Patricia Hamilton** *after it. She starts to return to the game offstage but halts, looks at the ball in her hand, and to someone offstage . . .*

Patricia   Why are we doing this? Come let's talk, I hate these games.

Mrs Karen Frick *enters. She is in her sixties, very thin, eyeglasses, wispy hair.*

Patricia   I said I'm quitting.

Karen *stares at the paddle.*

Patricia   Well, never mind. (*Studies her watch.*) You're very good.

Karen   My sister-in-law taught me. She used to be a stewardess on the *Queen Mary*. She could even play when the ship was rocking. But she never married.

Patricia   Here, put it down, dear.

Karen *passively gives up the paddle, then stands there looking uncomfortable.*

Patricia   I'm going to lie down in my room; come in if you like.

Karen   Hardly anyone ever seems to come out here.

Patricia   They don't like exercise, they're too depressed.

They enter the bedroom. **Patricia** *lies down. The* **Patient** *in the other bed does not stir and no attention is paid to her.*

Patricia   Don't feel obliged to say anything if you . . .

Karen   I get sick to my stomach just looking at a boat. Does your husband hunt?

Patricia   Sit down. Relax yourself. You don't have to talk. Although I think you're doing a little better than yesterday.

Karen   Oh, I like talking with you. (*Explaining herself timorously; indicating offstage – and very privately* . . .) I should go out – he doesn't like being kept waiting, don't y'know.

Patricia   Why are you so afraid? He might start treasuring you more if you make him wait a little. Come, sit.

Karen *adventurously sits at the foot of the bed, glancing about nervously.*

Patricia   Men are only big children, you know – give them a chocolate soda every day and pretty soon it doesn't mean a thing to them. (*Looks at her watch again.*) Only reason I'm nervous is that I can't decide whether to go home today. – But you mustn't mention it, will you?

Karen   Mention . . . ?

Patricia   About my pills. I haven't told anybody yet.

Karen *looks a bit blank.*

Patricia   Well never mind.

Karen   Oh! You mean not taking them.

Patricia   But you mustn't mention it, will you. The doctor would be very upset.

Karen   And how long has it been?

Patricia   Twenty-one days today. It's the longest I've been clean in maybe fifteen years. I can hardly believe it.

Karen   Are you Baptist?

Patricia   Baptist? No, we're more Methodist. But the church I'd really love hasn't been invented yet.

Karen (*charmed, slavishly interested*)   How would it be?

Patricia (*begins to describe it, breaks off*)   I can't describe it. (*A sigh of lostness.*) I was raised Lutheran, of course. – But I often go to the Marble Baptist Church on Route 91? I've gotten to like that minister. – You hear what I'm saying, don't you?

Karen *looks at her nervously trying to remember.*

Patricia   I must say it's kind of relaxing talking to you, Karen, knowing that you probably won't remember too much. But you'll come out of it all right, you're just a little scared, aren't you. – But who isn't?

Slight pause.

Doctor Rockwell is not going to believe I'm doing better without medication but I really think something's clicked inside me. (*A deep breath.*) I even seem to be breathing easier. And I'm not feeling that sort of fuzziness in my head. – It's like some big bird has been hovering over me for fifteen years, and suddenly it's flown away.

Karen   I can't stand dead animals, can you?

Patricia   Well just insist that he has to stop hunting! You don't have to stand for that, you're a *person*.

Karen   Well, you know, men like to . . .

Patricia   Not all – I've known some lovely men. Not many, but a few. This minister I mentioned? He came one day this summer and sat with me on our porch . . . and we had ice cream and talked for over an hour. You know, when he left his previous church they gave him a Pontiac Grand Am. He made me realize something; he said that I seem to be in like a constant state of prayer. And it's true; every once in a while it stops me short, realizing it. It's like inside me I'm almost continually talking to the Lord. (*Deeply excited, but suppressing it.*) I tell you truthfully, if I can really come out of this I'm going to . . . I don't know what . . . fall in love with God. I think I have already.

Karen   You're really beautiful.

Patricia   Oh no, dear, I'm a torn-off rag of my old self. The pills put ten years on my face. If he was a Jew or Italian or even Irish he'd be suing these doctors, but Yankees never sue, you know. Although I have to say the only thing he's been right about is medication.

Karen   Your husband against pills?

Patricia   Fanatical. But of course he can stick his head out the window and go high as a kite on a breath of fresh air. (*Looks at her watch.*)

Karen   I really think you're extremely attractive.

Patricia   No-no dear, although I did win the county beauty pageant when I was nineteen. But if you're talking beauty you should have seen my mother. She only died two years ago, age eighty-nine but I still haven't gotten over it. On the beach, right into her seventies, people would still be staring at her – she had an unbelievable bust right up to the end.

Karen   I cut this finger once in a broken Coke machine. But we never sued.

Patricia   Did your conversation always jump around? Because it could be your pills, believe me; the soul belongs to God, we're not supposed to be stuffing Prozac into His Mouth.

Karen   I have a cousin who went right through the windshield and she didn't get a cent.

Slight pause.

And it was five below zero out.

Slight pause.

Her husband's Norwegian.

Patricia   Look, dear, I know you're trying but don't feel you have to speak.

Karen   No, I like speaking to you. Is he Baptist too, your husband?

Patricia   I said Methodist. But he's more Episcopal. But he'll go to any church, if it's raining.

Slight pause. A deepening agitation.

I just don't know whether to tell him yet.

Karen   What?

Patricia   That I'm off everything.

Karen   But he'll like that, won't he?

Patricia   Oh yes. But he's going to be doubtful. – Which I am, too, let's face it – I've been on one medication or another for almost twenty years. But I do feel a thousand per cent better. And I really have no idea how it happened. (*Shakes her head.*) Dear God, when I think of him hanging in there all these years . . . I'm so ashamed. But at the same time he's absolutely refused to make any money, every one of our children has had to work since they could practically write their names. I can't be expected to applaud, exactly. (*Presses her eyes.*) I guess sooner or later you just have to stand up and say, 'I'm normal, I made it.' But it's like standing on top of a stairs and there's no stairs. (*Staring ahead.*)

Karen   I think I'd better go out to him. Should I tell your husband you're coming out?

Patricia   I think I'll wait a minute.

Karen (*stands*)   He seems very nice.

Patricia   I'll tell you the truth, dear – I've put him through hell and I know it . . . (*Tears threaten her.*) I know I have to stop blaming him; it came to me like a visitation two weeks ago, I-must-not-blame-Leroy-any more. And it's amazing, I lost all desire for medication, I could feel it leaving me like a . . . like a ghost.

Slight pause.

It's just that he's got really well-to-do relatives and he simply will not accept anyone's help. I mean you take the Jews, the Italians, Irish – they've got their Italian-Americans, Irish-Americans, Hispanic-Americans – they stick together and help each other. But you ever hear of Yankee-Americans? Not on your life. Raise his taxes, rob him blind, the Yankee'll just sit there all alone getting sadder and sadder. – But I'm not going to think about it any more.

Karen   You have a very beautiful chin.

Patricia   Men with half his ability riding around in big expensive cars and now for the second Easter Sunday in a row his rear end collapsed.

Karen   I think my license must have expired.

Patricia (*a surge of deep anger*)   I refuse to ride around in a nine-year-old Chevrolet which was bought second-hand in the first place!

Karen   They say there are only three keys for all General Motors cars. You suppose that's possible?

Patricia (*peremptorily now*)   Believe me dear, whatever they tell you, you have got to cut down the medication. It could be what's making your mind jump around . . .

Karen   No, it's that you mentioned Chevrolet, which is General Motors, you see.

Patricia   Oh . . . Well, let's just forget about it.

Slight pause.

Although you're probably right – here you're carefully locking your car and some crook is walking around with the same keys in his pocket. But everything's a fake, we all know that.

Karen (*facing* **Patricia** *again*)   I guess that would be depressing.

Patricia   No, that's not what depressed me . . .

Karen   No, I meant him refusing to amount to anything and then spending money on banjo lessons.

Patricia   Did I tell you that? – I keep forgetting what I told you because I never know when you're listening. (*Holds out her hand.*) Here we go again. (*Grasps her hand to stop the shaking.*)

Karen   – You sound like you had a wonderful courtship.

Patricia   Oh Karen, everyone envied us, we were the handsomest pair in town; and I'm not boasting, believe me. (*Breaks off; watches her hand shake and covers it again.*) I just don't want to have to come back here again, you see. I don't think

I could bear that. (*Grips her hand, moving about.*) I simply have to think positively. But it's unbelievable – he's seriously talking about donating his saw and chisel collection to the museum! – some of those tools are as old as the United States, they might be worth a fortune! – But I'm going to look ahead, that's all, just as straight ahead as a highway.

Slight pause.

Karen   I feel so ashamed.

Patricia   For Heaven's sakes, why? You've got a right to be depressed. There's more people in hospitals because of depression than any other disease.

Karen   Is that true?

Patricia   Of course! Anybody with any sense has got to be depressed in this country. Unless you're really rich, I suppose. Don't let him shame you, dear.

Karen   No . . . it's that you have so many thoughts.

Patricia   Oh. Well, you can have thoughts, too – just remember your soul belongs to God and you mustn't be shoving pills into His mouth.

Slight pause.

Karen   We're rich, I think.

Patricia (*quickly interested*) . . . Really rich?

Karen   He's got the oil delivery now, and of course he always had the fertilizer and the Chevy dealership, and of course the lumber yard and all. And Izuzus now.

Patricia   What's Izuzus?

Karen   It's a Japanese car.

Patricia   . . . I'll just never catch up.

Karen   We go to Arkansas in the spring.

Patricia   Arkansas?

Karen   For the catfish. It's where I broke down. But I can't help it, the sight of catfish makes me want to vomit. Not that I was trying to . . . you know . . . do anything. I just read the instructions on the bottle wrong. Do you mind if I ask you something?

Patricia   I hope it's nothing personal, is it?

Karen   Well, I don't know.

Patricia   . . . Well go ahead, what is it?

Karen   Do you shop in the A&P or Stop & Shop?

Patricia   . . . I'm wondering if you've got the wrong medication. But I guess you'll never overdose – you vomit at the drop of a hat. It may be your secret blessing.

Karen   – He wants to get me out of the house more, but it's hard to make up my mind where.

Patricia   Well . . . A&P is good. Or Stop & Shop. More or less. Kroger's is good for fish sometimes.

Karen   Which do you like best? I'll go where you go.

Patricia   You're very flattering. (*Stands, in excitement.*) It's amazing – I'm really beginning to feel wonderful, maybe I ought to go home with him today. I mean what does it come down to, really? – it's simply a question of confidence . . .

Karen   I wish we could raise some vegetables like we did on the farm. Do you?

Patricia   Oh, he raises things in our yard. Healthy things like salsify and collards – and kale. You ever eat kale?

Karen   I can't remember kale.

Patricia   You might as well salt your shower curtain and chop it up with a tomato.

Karen   – So . . . meats are . . . which? – A&P?

Patricia   No. Meats are Stop & Shop. I'm really thinking I might go home today. It's just not his fault. I have to remember that . . .

Karen   But staples?

Patricia   What? – Oh. Stop & Shop.

Karen   Then what's A&P for?

Patricia   Vegetables.

Karen   Oh right. And Krogers?

Patricia   Why don't you just forget Krogers.

Karen (*holds up five fingers, bends one at a time . . .*)   Then Stop & Shop . . .

Patricia   Maybe it's that you're trying to remember three things. Whyn't you just do A&P and Stop & Shop?

Slight pause.

Karen   I kind of liked Krogers.

Patricia   Then go to Krogers, for heaven's sake!

Karen   Well, I guess I'll go out to him. (*Moves to go. Halts.*) I hope you aren't really leaving today, are you?

Patricia (*higher tension*)   I'm deciding.

Karen   Well . . . here I go, I guess. (*Halts again.*) I meant to tell you, I kind of like the banjo. It's very good with tap-dancing.

Patricia   Tap-dancing.

Karen   There's a tap teacher lives in our road.

Patricia   You tap-dance?

Karen   Well John rented a video of Ginger Rogers and Fred Astaire, and I kind of liked it. I can sing 'Cheek to Cheek'? Would you like to hear it?

Patricia   Sure, go ahead – this is certainly a surprise.

Karen (*sings in a frail voice*) 'Heaven, I'm in heaven, and the cares that clung around me through the week . . . '

Patricia   That's beautiful, Karen! Listen, what exactly does Doctor Rockwell say about you?

Karen   Well, he says it's quite common when a woman is home alone all day.

Patricia   What's common?

Karen   Someone moving around in the next room?

Patricia   Oh, I see. – You have any idea who it is?

Karen   My mother. – My husband might bring my tap shoes and tails . . . but he probably forgot. I have a high hat and shorts too. And a walking stick? But would they allow dancing in here?

Patricia   They might. But of course the minute they see you enjoying yourself they'll probably try to knock you out with a pill.

Karen *makes to go, stalls and halts again.*

Karen   Did your mother like you?

Patricia   Oh yes. We were all very close. Didn't yours?

Karen   No. She left the whole farm to her cousin. Tell about your family, can you? Were they really all blond?

Patricia   Oh as blond as the tassels on Golden Bantam corn . . . everybody'd turn and look when we went by. My mother was perfection. We all were, I guess. (*With a chuckle.*) You know, we had a flat roof extending from the house over the garage, and mother and my sisters and me – on the first warm spring days we used to sunbathe out there.

Karen (*covering her mouth*)   No! You mean nude?

Patricia   Nudity doesn't matter that much in Sweden, and we were all brought up to love the sun. And we'd near die laughing because the minute we dropped our robes – you know how quiet a town Grenville is – you could hear the footsteps going up to the clock tower over the Presbyterian Church, and we pretended not to notice but that little narrow tower was just packed with Presbyterians.

Karen   Good lord!

Patricia   We'd stretch out and pretend not to see a thing. And then my mother'd sit up suddenly and point at the steeple and yell, 'Boo!' And they'd all go running down the stairs like mice!

They both enjoy the laugh.

Karen   I think your husband's very good-looking, isn't he?

Patricia   He is, but my brothers . . . I mean the way they stood, and walked . . . and their teeth! Charles won the All-New England golf tournament, and Buzz came within a tenth of an inch of the gold medal in the pole vault – that was in the Tokyo Olympics.

Karen   My! Do you still get together much?

Patricia   Oh, they're all gone now.

Karen   Moved away?

Patricia   No . . . dead.

Karen   Oh my. They overstrain?

Patricia   Buzz hung himself on his wife's closet door.

Karen   Oh my!

Patricia   Eight days later Charles shot himself on his tractor.

Karen (*softly*)   Oh my. Did they leave a note or anything?

Patricia   No. But we all knew what it was.

Karen   Can you say?

Patricia   Disappointment. We were all brought up expecting to be wonderful, and . . . (*Breaks off with a shrug.*) just wasn't.

Karen   Well . . . here I go.

Karen *exits.* **Patricia** *stares ahead for a moment in a blankly reminiscent mood. Now she looks at her face in a mirror, smoothing wrinkes away . . .*

Leroy *enters.*

Patricia   I was just coming out.

Leroy   'Cause Mrs Frick . . .

Patricia (*cuts him off by drawing his head down and stroking his cheek. And in soft but faintly patronizing tone . . .*)   I was just coming out, Leroy. You don't have to repeat everything. Come, sit with me and let's not argue.

Leroy   . . . How's your day been?

She is still moved by her brothers' memory; also, she hasn't received something she hoped for from him. She shrugs and turns her head away.

Patricia   I've had worse.

Leroy   Did you wash your hair?

Patricia (*pleased he noticed*)   How can you tell?

Leroy   Looks livelier. Is that nail polish?

Patricia   M-hm.

Leroy   Good. You're looking good, Patty.

Patricia   I'm feeling better. Not completely but a lot.

Leroy (*nods approvingly*)   Great! Did he change your medication or something?

Patricia   No.

Leroy   Something different about you.

Patricia (*mysteriously excited*)   You think so?

Leroy   Your eyes are clearer. You seem more like you're . . . connecting.

Patricia   I am, I think. But I warn you, I'm nervous.

Leroy   That's okay. Your color is more . . . I don't know . . .
vigorous.

Patricia   Is it? (*She touches her face.*)

Leroy   You look almost like years ago . . .

Patricia   Something's happened but I don't want to talk
about it yet.

Leroy   Really? Like what?

Patricia (*instant resistance*)   I just said I . . .

Leroy   Okay (*Goes to a window.*) – It looks like rain outside,
but we can walk around if you like. They've got a beautiful
tulip bed down there; the colors really shine in this gray light.
Reds and purple and whites, and a gray. Never saw a tulip be
that kind of gray.

Patricia   How's Amelia's leg? Are you getting her to change
her bandage?

Leroy   Yes. But she'd better stop thinking she can drive a car.

Patricia   Well, why don't you tell her?

Leroy (*a little laugh*)   That'll be the day, won't it, when she
starts listening to her father.

Patricia (*a softness despite her language*)   She might if you laid
down the law without just complaining. And if she could hear
something besides disappointment in your voice.

Leroy   She's learned to look down at me, Patty, you know
that.

Patricia (*strongly, but nearly a threat of weeping*)   Well I hope
you're not blaming me for that.

Leroy (*he holds back, stands silent. Then puffs out his cheeks and
blows, shaking his head with a defensive grin*)   Not my day, I see.

Patricia   Maybe it could have been.

Leroy   I was looking forward to telling you something.

Patricia   What.

Leroy   I got Harrelson to agree to twelve-thousand-five for the altar.

Patricia   There, you see – and you were so glad to accept eight! I told you . . . !

Leroy   I give you all the credit. I finally got it through my thick skull, I said to myself, okay, you are slower than most, but quality's got a right to be slow. And he didn't make a peep – twelve thousand, five hundred dollars.

She looks at him, immensely sad.

– Well why do you look so sad?

Patricia   Come here.

Draws him down, kisses him.

I'm glad . . . I started to think of all these years wasted trying to get you to charge enough, but I've decided to keep looking straight ahead, not back – I'm very glad you got the twelve. You've done a wonderful thing.

Leroy (*excited*)   Listen, what has he got you on?

Patricia   Well I'm still a long way from perfect, but I . . .

Leroy   Patty, nothing's perfect except a hot bath.

Patricia   It's nothing to joke about. I told you I'm nervous, I'm not used to . . . to . . .

Leroy   He changed your medication didn't he?

Patricia   I just don't want you to think I have no problems anymore.

Leroy   Oh, I'd never think that, Patty. Has he put you on something new?

Patricia   *He* hasn't done anything.

Pause.

Leroy   Okay, I'll shut up.

She sweeps her hair back; he silently observes her. Then . . .

. . . This Mr Frick handles oil burners; I don't know if I can trust him but he says he'd give me a good buy. We could use a new burner.

Patricia   What would you say if I said I'm thinking of coming home.

Leroy (*a pause filled with doubt*)   You are? When?

Patricia   Maybe next Thursday. For good.

Leroy   Uh-huh.

Patricia   You don't sound very positive.

Leroy   You know you're the only one can make that decision, Pat. You want to come home I'm always happy to take you home.

Slight pause.

Patricia   I feel if I could look ahead just the right amount I'd be all right.

Leroy   What do you mean?

Patricia   I realized something lately; when I'm home I have a tendency – especially in the afternoons when everybody's out and I'm alone – I look very far ahead. What I should do is only look ahead a little bit, like to the evening or the next day. And then it's all right. It's when I start looking years ahead . . .

Slight pause.

You once told me why you think I got sick. I've forgotten . . . what did you say?

Leroy   What do I really know about it, Pat?

Patricia   Why do you keep putting yourself down? – you've got to stop imitating your father. There are things you know very well. – Remind me what you said . . . Why am I sick?

Leroy   I always thought it was your family –

Patricia (*fingers pressing on her eyes*)   I want to concentrate.
Go on.

Leroy   They were so close, they were all over each other, and
you all had this – you know – very high opinion of yourselves;
each and every one of you was automatically going to go to
the head of the line just because your name was Sorgenson.
And life isn't that way, so you got sick.

Long pause; she stares, nodding.

Patricia   You've had no life at all have you.

Leroy   I wouldn't say that.

Patricia   I can't understand how I never saw it.

Leroy   Why? – it's been great watching the kids growing up;
and I've had some jobs I've enjoyed . . .

Patricia   But not your wife.

Leroy   It's a long time since I blamed you, Pat. It's your
upbringing.

Patricia   Well I could blame yours too, couldn't I.

Leroy   You sure could.

Patricia   I mean this constant optimism is very irritating
when you're fifty times more depressed than I am.

Leroy   Now Patty, you know that's not . . .

Patricia   You are depressed, Leroy! Because you're scared of
people, you really don't trust anyone, and that's incidentally
why you never made any money. You could have set the world
on fire but you can't bear to work along with other human
beings.

Leroy   The last human being I took on to help me tried to
steal my half-inch Stanley chisel.

Patricia   You mean you *think* he tried . . .

Leroy   I didn't think anything, I found it in his toolbox. And
that's an original Stanley, not the junk they sell today.

Patricia   So what!

Leroy   So what? – that man has three grandchildren! And he's a Chapman – that's one of the oldest upstanding families in the county.

Patricia (*emphatically, her point proved*)   Which is why you're depressed.

Leroy (*laughs*)   I'm not, but why shouldn't I be? – a Chapman stealing a chisel? I mean God Almighty, they've had generals in that family, secretaries of state or some goddam thing. Anyway, if I'm depressed it's from something that happened, not something I imagine.

Patricia   I feel like a log that keeps bumping against another log in the middle of the river.

Leroy   Boy, you're a real roller-coaster. We were doing great there for a minute, what got us off on this?

Patricia   I can't be at peace when I know you are full of denial, and that's saying it straight.

Leroy   What denial? – (*Laughs.*) You want me to say I'm a failure?

Patricia   That is not what I . . .

Leroy   Hey, I know what – I'll get a bumper sticker printed up – 'The driver of this car is a failure!' – I betcha I could sell a hundred million of them . . . (*A sudden fury.*) . . . Or maybe I should just drive out on a tractor and shoot myself!

Patricia   That's a terrible thing to say to me, Leroy!

Leroy   Well I'm sorry, Patty, but I'm not as dumb as I look – I'll never win if I have to compete against your brothers!

Patricia (*chastened for the moment*)   I did not say you're a failure.

Leroy   I didn't mean to yell; I'm sorry. I know you don't mean to sound like you do, sometimes.

Patricia (*unable to retrieve . . .*)   I said nothing about a failure. (*On the verge of weeping.*)

Leroy   It's okay, maybe I am a failure; but in my opinion no more than the rest of this country.

Patricia   What happened? – I thought this visit started off so nicely.

Leroy   Maybe you're not used to being so alert; you've been so lethargic for a long time, you know.

She moves; he watches her.

I'm sure of it, Pat, if you could only find two ounces of trust I know we could still have a life.

Patricia   I know.

Slight pause, she fights downs tears.

What did you have in mind, exactly, when you said it was my upbringing?

Leroy   I don't know . . . I had a flash of your father, that time long ago when we were sitting on your porch . . . we were getting things ready for our wedding . . . and right in front of you he turns to me cool as a cucumber and says, (*Through laughter, imitating Swedish accent.*) 'No Yankee will ever be good enough for a Swedish girl.' I nearly fell off into the rose bushes.

Patricia (*laughs with a certain delight*)   Well, he was old-fashioned . . .

Leroy (*laughing*).   Yeah, a real old-fashioned welcome into the family!

Patricia   Well, the Yankees *were* terrible to us.

Leroy   That's a hundred years ago, Pat.

Patricia (*starting to anger*)   You shouldn't keep denying this! – They paid them fifty cents a week and called us dumb Swedes with strong backs and weak minds and did nothing but make us ridiculous.

Leroy   But Patty, if you walk around town today there isn't a good piece of property that isn't owned by Swedes.

Patricia   But that's now.

Leroy   Well when are we living?

Patricia   We were treated like animals, some Yankee doctors wouldn't come out to a Swedish home to deliver a baby . . .

Leroy (*laughs*)   Well, all I hope is that I'm the last Yankee so people can start living today instead of a hundred years ago.

Patricia   There was something else you said. About standing on line.

Leroy   On line?

Patricia   That you'll always be at the head of the line because . . . (*Breaks off.*)

Leroy   I'm the only one on it.

Patricia   . . . Is that really true? You do compete, don't you? You must, at least in your mind?

Leroy   Only with myself. We're really all on a one-person line, Pat. I learned that in these years.

Pause. She stares ahead.

Patricia   That's very beautiful. Where'd you get that idea?

Leroy   I guess I made it up, I don't know. It's up to you, Pat – if you feel you're ready, let's go home. Now or Thursday or whenever. What about medication?

Patricia (*makes herself ready*)   I wasn't going to tell you for another week or two, till I'm absolutely rock-sure – I've stopped taking anything for . . . this is twenty-one days.

Leroy   *Anything?* (*She nods with a certain suspense.*) My God, Patty. And you feel all right?

Patricia   . . . I haven't felt this way in – fifteen years. I've no idea why, but I forgot to take anything, and I slept right through till morning, and I woke up and it was like . . . I'd been blessed during the night. And I haven't had anything since.

Leroy   Did I tell you or didn't I!

Patricia   But it's different for you. You're not addictive . . .

Leroy   But didn't I tell you all that stuff is poison? I'm just flying, Patty.

Patricia (*clasps her hands to steady herself*)   But I'm afraid about coming home. I don't know if I'm jumping the gun. I *feel* I could, but . . .

Leroy   Well let's talk about it. Is it a question of trusting yourself? Because I think if you've come this far . . .

Patricia   Be quiet a minute! (*She holds his hand.*) Why have you stayed with me?

Leroy (*laughs*)   God knows!

Patricia   I've been very bad to you sometimes, Leroy, I really see that now. (*Starting to weep.*) Tell me the truth; in all these years, have you gone to other women? I wouldn't blame you, I just want to know.

Leroy   Well, I've thought of it but I never did anything.

Patricia (*looking deeply into his eyes*)   You really haven't, have you?

Leroy   No.

Patricia   Why?

Leroy   I just kept hoping you'd come out of this.

Patricia   But it's been so long.

Leroy   I know.

Patricia   Even when I'd . . . throw things at you?

Leroy   Uh-uh.

Patricia   Like that time with the roast?

Leroy   Well, that's one time I came pretty close. But I knew it was those damned pills, not you.

Patricia   But why would you be gone night after night? That was a woman, wasn't it.

Leroy   No. Some nights I went over to the library basement to practice banjo with Phil Palumbo. Or to Manny's Diner for some donuts and talk to the fellas.

Patricia (*slightest tinge of suspicion*)   There are fellas there at *night*?

Leroy   Sure; working guys, mostly young single fellas. But some with wives. You know – have a beer, watch TV.

Patricia   And women?

Leroy (*a short beat*)   – You know, Pat – and I'm not criticizing – but wouldn't it be better for you to try believing a person instead of trying not to believe?

Patricia   I'm just wondering if you know . . . there's lots of women would love having you. But you probably don't know that, do you?

Leroy   Sure I do.

Patricia   You know lots of women would love to have you?

Leroy   . . . Well, yes, I know that.

Patricia   Really. How do you know that?

Leroy (*his quick, open laugh*)   I can tell.

Patricia   Then what's keeping you? Why don't you move out?

Leroy   Pat, you're torturing me.

Patricia   I'm trying to find myself!

She moves on stress, warding off an explosion. There is angry resentment in his voice.

Leroy   I'd remember you happy and loving – that's what kept me; as long ago as that is now, I'd remember how you'd pull on your stockings and get a little make-up on and pin up your hair . . . When you're positive about life there's just nobody like you. Nobody. Not in life, not in the movies, not on TV.

Slight pause.

But I'm not going to deny it – if it wasn't for the kids I probably *would* have gone.

She is silent, but loaded with something unspoken.

You're wanting to tell me something, aren't you?

Patricia   – I know what a lucky woman I've been.

Leroy (*he observes her*)   – What is it, you want me to stop coming to see you for a while? Please tell me, Pat; there's something on your mind.

Pause. She forces it out.

Patricia   I know I shouldn't feel this way, but I'm not too sure I could stand it, knowing that it's never going to . . . I mean will it ever change any more?

Leroy   You mean – is it ever going to be 'wonderful'.

She looks at him, estimating.

Well – no, I guess this is pretty much it; although to me it's already wonderful – I mean the kids, and there are some clear New England mornings when you want to drink the air and the sunshine.

Patricia   You can make more out of a change in temperature than any human being I ever heard of – I can't live on weather!

Leroy   Pat we're getting old! This is just about as rich and handsome as I'm ever going to be and as good as you're ever going to look, so you want to be with me or not?

Patricia   I don't want to fool either of us . . . I can't bear it when you can't pay the bills . . .

Leroy   But I'm a carpenter – this is probably the way it's been for carpenters since they built Noah's ark. What do you want to do?

Patricia   I'm honestly not sure I could hold up. Not when I hear your sadness all the time and your eyes are full of disappointment. You seem . . . (*Breaks off.*)

Leroy   . . . How do I seem?

Patricia   I shouldn't say it . . .

Leroy   . . . Beaten. Like it's all gone by.

She doesn't contradict.

(*Hurt, but holding on*) All right, Patty, then I might as well say it – I don't think you *ever* had a medical problem; you have an attitude problem . . .

Patricia   My problem is spiritual.

Leroy   Okay, I don't mind calling it spiritual.

Patricia   Well that's a new note; I thought these ministers were all quacks.

Leroy   Not at all; but the ones who make house calls with women, eating up all the ice cream, are not my idea of spiritual.

Patricia   *You* know what spiritual is?

Leroy   For me? Sure. Ice skating.

Patricia   Ice skating is spiritual?

Leroy   Yes, and skiing! To me spiritual is whatever makes me forget myself and feel happy to be alive. Like even a well-sharpened saw, or a perfect compound joint.

Patricia   Maybe this is why we can't get along – spiritual is nothing you can see, Leroy.

Leroy   Really! Then why didn't God make everything invisible! We are in this world and you're going to have to find some way to love it!

Her eyes are filling with tears.

Pounding on me is not going to change anything to wonderful, Patty.

She seems to be receiving him.

I'll say it again, because it's the only thing that's kept me from going crazy – you just have to love this world.

He comes to her, takes her hand.

Come home. Maybe it'll take a while but I really believe you can make it.

Uncertainty filling her face . . .

All right, don't decide now, I'll come back Thursday and we'll see then.

Patricia   Where are you going now?

Leroy   For my banjo lesson. I'm learning a new number. – I'll play it for you if you want to hear it.

Patricia (*hesitates, then kisses him*)   Couldn't you do it on guitar?

Leroy   It's not the same on guitar.

He goes to his banjo case and opens it.

Patricia   But banjo sounds so picky.

Leroy   But that's what's good about it, it's clean, like a toothpick . . .

Enter the **Fricks**.

Leroy   Oh hi, Mrs Frick.

Karen   He brought my costume. Would you care to see it? – (*To* **Frick**.) This is her – Mrs Hamilton.

Frick   Oh! How do you do?

Karen   This is my husband.

Patricia   How do you do?

Frick   She's been telling me all about you. (*Shaking* **Patricia**'s *hand*.) I want to say that I'm thankful to you.

Patricia   Really? What for?

Frick   Well what she says you've been telling her. About her attitude and all.

Karen (*to* **Patricia**)   Would you like to see my costume? I also have a blue one but . . .

Frick (*overriding her*)   By the way, I'm Frick Lumber, I recognized your husband right away . . .

Karen   Should I put it on?

Patricia   Sure, put it on!

Leroy *starts tuning his banjo.*

Frick (*to* **Patricia**)   All it is is a high hat and shorts, y'know . . . nothing much to it.

Karen (*to* **Frick**)   Shouldn't I?

Patricia   Why not, for Heaven's sake?

Frick   Go ahead, if they want to see it. (*Laughs to* **Patricia**.) She found it in a catalogue. I think it's kinda silly at her age, but I admit I'm a conservative kind of person . . .

Karen (*cutting him off, deeply embarrassed*)   I'll only be a minute. (*She starts out, and stops, and to* **Patricia**.) You really think I should?

Patricia   Of course!

Frick (*suppressing an angry embarrassment*)   Karen, honey, if you're going to do it, do it.

Karen *exits with valise.* **Leroy** *tunes his instrument.*

Frick   The slightest decision, she's got to worry it into the ground. – But I have to tell you, it's years since I've seen this much life in her, she's like day and night. What exactly'd you say to her? (*To* **Leroy**, *thumbing toward* **Patricia**.) She says she just opened up her eyes.

Leroy (*surprised*)   Patricia?

Frick   I have to admit, it took me a while to realize it's a sickness . . .

Patricia   You're not the only one.

Frick   Looked to me like she was just favoring herself; I mean the woman has everything, what right has she got to start shooting blanks like that? I happen to be a great believer in self-discipline, started from down below sea level myself, sixty acres of rocks and swampland is all we had. That's why I'm so glad that somebody's talked to her with your attitude.

Patricia (*vamping for time*)   What . . . what attitude do you mean?

Frick   Just that you're so . . . so positive. (**Leroy** *looks up at* **Patricia** *thunderstruck.*) She says you made her realize all the things she could be doing instead of mooning around all day . . .

Patricia   Well I think being positive is the only way.

Frick   That's just what I tell her . . .

Patricia   But you have to be careful not to sound so disappointed in her.

Frick   I sound disappointed?

Patricia   In a way, I think. – She's got to feel treasured, you see.

Frick   I appreciate that, but the woman can stand in one place for half an hour at a time practically without moving.

Patricia   Well that's the sickness, you see.

Frick   I realize that. But she won't even go shopping . . .

Patricia   You see? You're sounding disappointed in her.

Frick (*angering*)   I am not disappointed in her! I'm just telling you the situation!

Patricia   Mr Frick, she's standing under a mountain a mile high – you've got to help her over it. That woman has very big possibilities!

Frick   Think so?

Patricia   Absolutely.

Frick   I hope you're right. (*To* **Leroy**, *indicating* **Patty**.) You don't mind my saying it, you could do with a little of her optimism.

Leroy (*turns from* **Patricia**, *astonished*)   Huh?

Frick (*to* **Patricia**, *warmly*)   Y'know, she made me have a little platform built down the cellar, with a big full-length mirror so she could see herself dance.

Patricia   But do you spend time watching her . . .

Frick   Well she says not to till she's good at it.

Patricia   That's because she's terrified of your criticism.

Frick   But I haven't made any criticism.

Patricia   But do you like tap-dancing?

Frick   Well I don't know, I never thought about it one way or another.

Patricia   Well that's the thing, you see. It happens to mean a great deal to her . . .

Frick   I'm for it, I don't mean I'm not for it. But don't tell me you think it's normal for a woman her age to be getting out of bed two, three in the morning and start practicing.

Patricia   Well maybe she's trying to get you interested in it. Are you?

Frick   In tap-dancing? Truthfully, no.

Patricia   Well there you go . . .

Frick   Well we've got a lot of new competition in our fuel oil business . . .

Patricia   Fuel oil!

Frick   I've got seven trucks on the road that I've got to keep busy . . .

Patricia   Well there you go, maybe that's why your wife is in here.

Frick (*visibly angering*)   Well, I can't be waked up at two o'clock in the morning and be any good next day, now can I. She's not normal.

Patricia   Normal! They've got whole universities debating what's normal. Who knows what's normal, Mr Frick?

Frick   You mean getting out of bed at two o'clock in the morning and putting on a pair of tap shoes is a common occurrence in this country? I don't think so. – But I didn't mean to argue when you're . . . not feeling well.

Patricia   I've never felt better.

She turns away, and **Frick** *looks with bewildered surprise to* **Leroy**, *who returns him a look of suppressed laughter.*

Frick   You sure know how to turn somebody inside out.

Karen *enters; she is dressed in satin shorts, a tail-coat, a high hat, tap shoes, and as they turn to look at her, she pulls out a collapsible walking stick, and strikes a theatrical pose.*

Patricia   Well now, don't you look great!

Karen (*desperate for reassurance*)   You really like it?

Leroy   That looks terrific!

Patricia   Do a step!

Karen   I don't have my tape. (*Turns to* **Frick**, *timorously.*) But if you'd sing 'Swanee River . . .'

Frick   Oh Karen for God's sake!

Patricia   I can sing it . . .

Karen   He knows my speed. Please, John . . . just for a
minute.

Frick   All right, go ahead. (*Unhappily, he sings.*)
   'Way down upon the Swanee River . . .'

Karen   Wait, you're too fast . . .

Frick (*slower and angering*)
   'Way – down – upon – the – Swanee River,
   Far, far away.
   That's where my heart is turning ever . . . ' (*Etc.*)

Karen *taps out her number, laboriously but for a short stretch with a
promise of grace.* **Frick** *continues singing.*

Patricia   Isn't she wonderful?

Leroy   Hey, she's great!

Karen *dances a bit more boldly, a joyous freedom starting into her.*

Patricia   She's marvellous! Look at her, Mr Frick.

A hint of the sensuous in **Karen** *now:* **Frick**, *embarrassed, uneasily
avoids more than a glance at his wife.*

Frick
   ' . . . everywhere I roam . . . '

Patricia   Will you look at her!

Frick (*hard-pressed, explodes*)   I am looking at her, goddammit!

*This astonishing furious shout, his reddened face, stops everything. A look
of fear is on* **Karen**'s *face.*

Karen (*apologetically to* **Patricia**)   He was looking at me . . .
(*To* **Frick**.) She didn't mean you weren't looking, she meant . . .

Frick (*rigidly repressing his anger and embarrassment*)   I've got to
run along now.

Karen   I'm so sorry, John, but she . . .

Frick (*rigidly*)   Nothing to be sorry about, dear. Very nice to
have met you folks.

Ht starts to exit. **Karen** *moves to interrupt him.*

Karen   Oh John, I hope you're not . . . going to be angry –

Frick   I'm just fine. (*He sees her despair coming on.*) What are you looking so sad about? – you danced great . . . (*She is immobile.*) I'm sorry to've raised my voice but it don't mean I'm disappointed, dear. You understand? (*A nervous glance toward* **Patricia**. *Stiffly, with enormous effort . . .*) You . . . you danced better than I ever saw you. (*She doesn't change.*) Now look here, Karen, I hope you don't feel I'm . . . disappointed or something, you hear . . ? 'Cause I'm not. And that's definite. (*She keeps staring at him.*) I'll try to make it again on Friday. – Keep it up.

He abruptly turns and exits.

Karen *stands perfectly still, staring at nothing.*

Patricia   Karen?

Karen *seems not to hear, standing there facing the empty door in her high hat and costume.*

Patricia   How about Leroy playing it for you? (*To* **Leroy**.) Play it.

Leroy   I could on the guitar, but I never did on this . . .

Patricia   Well couldn't you try it? – I don't know what *good* that thing is.

Leroy   Well here . . . let me see.

He picks out 'Swanee River' on banjo, but **Karen** *doesn't move.*

Patricia   There you go, Karen! Try it, I love your dancing! Come on . . . (*Sings.*)

'Way down upon the Swanee River . . . '

Karen *now breaks her motionlessly depressed mode and looks at* **Patricia**. **Leroy** *continues playing, humming along with it. His picking is getting more accurate . . .*

Patricia   Is it the right tempo? Tell him!

Karen (*very very softly*)   Could you play a little faster?

*Leroy speeds it up. With an unrelieved sadness, **Karen** goes into her number, does a few steps, but stops. **Leroy** gradually stops playing. **Karen** walks out. **Patricia** starts to follow her but gives it up and comes to a halt.*

*Leroy turns to **Patricia**, who is staring ahead. Now she turns to **Leroy**.*

He meets her gaze, his face filled with inquiry. He comes to her and stands there.

For a long moment neither of them moves. Then she reaches out and touches his face – there is a muted gratitude in her gesture.

She goes to a closet and takes a small overnight bag to the bed and puts her things into it.

Leroy watches her for a moment, then stows his banjo in its case, and stands waiting for her. She starts to put on a light coat. He comes and helps her into it.

Her face is charged with her struggle against her self-doubt.

Leroy (*laughs, but about to weep*)   Ready?

Patricia (*filling up*)   Leroy . . .

Leroy   One day at a time, Pat – you're already twenty-one ahead. Kids are going to be so happy to have you home.

Patricia   I can't believe it . . . I've had nothing.

Leroy   It's a miracle.

Patricia   Thank you.

Breaking through her own resistance, she draws him to her and kisses him. Grinning tauntingly . . .

That car going to get us home?

Leroy (*laughs*)   Stop picking on that car, it's all checked out!

They start towards the door, he carrying her bag and his banjo.

Patricia   Once you believe in something you just never know when to stop, do you?

Leroy   Well there's very little rust, and the new ones aren't half as well-built . . .

Patricia   Waste not, want not.

Leroy   Well I really don't *go* for those new Chevies . . .

She walks out, he behind her. Their voices are heard . . .

Patricia   Between the banjo and that car I've certainly got a whole lot to look forward to.

His laughter sounds down the corridor.

The woman on the bed stirs, then falls back and remains motionless. A stillness envelops the whole stage.

End.

Notes

page
4   *Ivy League jacket and slacks and shined brogues*: Leroy's clothes
    suggest a man with an élite, private university education.
    The Ivy League schools include Princeton, Harvard,
    Yale, Dartmouth, Columbia, the University of
    Pennsylvania, Cornell and Brown.
5   *Awful lot of colored*: by using the antiquated term 'colored'
    to refer to African-Americans, Frick shows his racial
    insensitivity and prejudice.
8   *When she started locking up everything I thought maybe it's these
    Negroes, you know?*: Negro, although more contemporary
    than the term 'colored' as a reference to African-
    Americans, has been widely considered offensive since
    the 1970s. When combined with the suggestion that
    'Negroes' have criminal tendencies, Frick shows himself
    to be both limited and exceedingly narrow-minded.
9   *Mine was never very optimistic. She's Swedish*: Leroy means
    this as a joke; he's playing on the stereotype of Swedish
    immigrants to the United States (and Scandinavians,
    generally) as being dour and pessimistic. This originates
    from both the cold climate they come from and the
    assumption that Swedish Lutheranism is often perceived
    as being a rigid form of Protestantism.
9   *Plus tips*: the idea of tipping the hospital staff
    characterises the Rogers Pavilion as a facility for the
    wealthy.
10 *Colonial Trust*: a name for a bank that suggests age and
    reliability.
10 *Contractor*: one who manages a large building project,
    rather than a workman who would do the actual labour.
11 *Descended from Alexander Hamilton*: one of the play's central
    ironies is Leroy's status as a descendant of Hamilton.

The main author of *The Federalist Papers*, a collection of essays which advocated passing of the United States Constitution, and George Washington's Secretary of the Treasury, Hamilton represented an authoritarian, pro-industrial view of American government. In other words, he is the Founding Father Leroy Hamilton would least admire.

12   *I'm renovating a colonial*: Leroy is working on a house that either dates from (or is built to reproduce) a home from the colonial period.

12   *Presbyterian Church*: the Presbyterians are a Protestant denomination who follow the teachings of John Calvin and John Knox. Now an established religious organisation in the United States, Presbyterians have strong roots in Calvinist reform traditions. This would include relatively spare church interiors, where Leroy's altar and its craftsmanship would be both visible and appreciated for its understated appearance.

13   *He was one of the most important Founding Fathers*: as a group, the Founding Fathers are generally understood to include the men who signed the Declaration of Independence in 1776 and those who constructed and approved the Constitution of the United States in 1787.

14   *It was something to do with his philosophy*: Hamilton's philosophy, expressed in *The Federalist Papers*, promoted the idea of a centralised government and an industrial economy, in contrast to Thomas Jefferson's agrarian and democratic vision of the new United States. Frick himself, as a capitalist, is strictly in the Hamiltonian mode.

14   *equality, or what kind of country*: Leroy's shorthand neatly encapsulates the ends of the ideological political spectrum. Either, he suggests, one favours the equality of all people or one subscribes to an élitist view that the country can be despoiled by 'the wrong sort'.

15   *Mimes thumb pridefully tucked into suspenders*: suspenders here means braces. For a moment, Leroy is playing the role of a portly, rich man.

15   *I'm only a dumb swamp Yankee*: while the term 'Yankee' has

a long history with both positive and negative connotations, the epithet 'swamp Yankee' has a specific, local meaning in Connecticut, Rhode Island and Massachusetts. According to Ruth Schell, who described the term for the journal *American Speech*, "'swamp Yankee" may be defined as "a rural New England dweller who abides today as a steadfast rustic and who is of Yankee stock that has endured in the New England area since the colonial days"'. While it might be considered pejorative when used by an outsider, Leroy's use of the term mixes in a bit of pride – it represents his values, as well as the values he rejects, such as material ambition.

16   *She used to be a stewardess on the* Queen Mary: the *Queen Mary* was a transatlantic liner in service between 1936 and 1967, operated by the Cunard Line. Karen's mention of her sister-in-law's service evokes an image of a particularly elegant means of travel while also suggesting that John Frick was not born into a wealthy family.

16   *Does your husband hunt?*: hunting in this context means pursuing game on foot, armed with a gun or rifle, usually in the woods.

17   *Are you Baptist?*: Karen and Patricia's exchange about Protestant denominations reads almost like a comedy routine, where the joke is the relative lack of distinction between them. Although many religious Americans remain life-long members of the churches they grew up in, others switch churches, and even denominations, quite frequently. Patricia's behaviour is not, in that sense, unusual.

17   *No, we're more Methodist*: the Methodist tradition comes from John Wesley's movement to reform the Anglican Church. In America, Methodists are associated with the three evangelical revival movements known as the Great Awakenings. As in England, Methodism was originally popular with working-class people, but that distinction no longer holds true in the United States.

17   *I was raised Lutheran, of course*: coming from a Swedish

family, a Lutheran church upbringing is nearly inevitable for Patricia. Lutheran theology can be distinguished from the Calvinist Reformed traditions by its emphasis on salvation through grace rather than predestination.

18 *Doctor Rockwell*: no doctors appear on stage in *The Last Yankee*, but this doctor's name suggests Patricia's belief that the doctors, through the drugs they prescribe, merely sedate patients. The name also invokes Norman Rockwell, the American painter well known for documenting small-town life on the covers of the *Saturday Evening Post* magazine.

18 *when he left his previous church they gave him a Pontiac Grand Am*: the Grand Am was a car first designed in the 1970s by General Motors, generally as a mid-sized coupé or sedan.

19 *Prozac*: the anti-depressant medication fluoxetine, manufactured by the Eli Lilly Corporation. Prozac is a selective serotonin reuptake inhibitor (SSRI). First introduced for sale in the United States in 1987, Prozac became both a medical and cultural phenomenon. At the time *The Last Yankee* was written, Prozac was probably the most talked-about psychiatric medication in America.

19 *But he's more Episcopal. But he'll go to any church, if it's raining*: the Episcopal Church is the American branch of the Anglican Communion, and hews closer to the teachings of the Church of England than any of the other denominations mentioned in the play. Patricia's comment about 'any church, if it's raining' suggests that Leroy's church attendance is casual, more motivated by practicality and convenience than belief.

20 *I mean you take the Jews, the Italians, Irish – they've got their Italian-Americans, Irish-Americans, Hispanic-Americans – they stick together and help each other. But you ever hear of Yankee-Americans?*: the idea of 'hyphenated Americans' originated in the late nineteenth century, and was originally a derogatory term indicating someone with split loyalties.

21   *his rear-end collapsed*: Patricia is talking, ironically, about
Leroy's car.

21   *nine-year-old Chevrolet*: Chevrolet is an American car built
by General Motors. As a reflection of the American love
affair with the automobile, Patricia assumes that driving
an older car, or buying a used one in the first place, is a
mark of poverty and, perhaps, even moral shame.

21   *only three keys for all General Motors cars*: Karen, whose
husband sells cars, seems unimpressed by the idea of
cars as a mark of success. Her comment reflects a view
of cars as a commodity rather than popular signifiers of
social status.

21   *spending money on banjo lessons*: the banjo was developed
by African slaves adapting traditional instruments to
new-world materials. It is principally used in African-
American traditional, bluegrass and country music
and, unlike the Spanish guitar or the violin family,
remains completely outside the classical music
repertory. Patricia seems to think playing the banjo
(much less spending money on the pursuit) is a low-
status hobby.

22   *just as straight ahead as a highway*: the open road has a
particular mystique in American culture, in that it leads
to new horizons and new opportunities. Limited access
highways, such as the federal interstate highway system,
carry additional metaphorical weight as symbols of
human ingenuity and freedom, particularly when they
cut through otherwise uninhabited landscapes.

22   *There's more people in hospitals because of depression than any
other disease*: this idea is among those that led Miller to
write *The Last Yankee*. In his essay 'About Theatre
Language', he expands on this line, adding '[in] life,
with such people, a high degree of objectification or
distancing exists, and the style of the play had to reflect
the fact that [depression sufferers] commonly know a
great deal about the social setting of the illness even as
they are unable to tear themselves free from it'.
Researchers have also discovered that women are more
likely than men to go to hospital for depression.

22   *He's got the oil delivery now, and of course he always had the fertilizer and the Chevy dealership, and of course the lumber yard and all. And Isuzu's now*: Karen's inventory of Frick's business interests means that the Fricks are rich by Patricia's standards. Not only do they have money, but Patricia takes this diverse commercial inventory as a symbol for the kind of ambition Leroy refuses to value. In the late 1980s, Isuzus were advertised in the United States through a series of television commercials featuring 'Joe Isuzu', a character who made wildly outsized and untrue claims about the cars. The commercials became a pop-culture sensation.

22   *We go to Arkansas in the spring*: Arkansas is a southern state bordering the Mississippi River, known for sport fishing. Literally and metaphorically, it is a long way from New England.

23   *Not that I was trying to . . . you know . . . do anything. I just read the instructions on the bottle wrong*: this is Karen's only allusion to the overdose of pills that has led to her being in hospital.

23   *Do you shop in the A&P or Stop & Shop*: both are grocery-store chains commonly found in New England.

23   *Krogers*: Kroger is another grocery chain. Based in Ohio, it can be found throughout the United States.

23   *Healthy things like salsify and collards – and kale*: Patricia not only dislikes these healthy greens because of their taste, but she also considers them to be foods grown and cooked by poor people. Collards, in particular, would seem out of place in New England as they are associated with southern home cooking.

24   *I kind of like the banjo. It's very good with tap-dancing*: Karen surprises Patricia by valuing forms of cultural expression Patricia feels should be beneath her. Karen's predilection for tap-dance marks her individuality. Tap-dance is the one thing she has that is separate from her husband's interests.

24   *Ginger Rogers and Fred Astaire*: Ginger Rogers and Fred Astaire popularised a dance style known as ballroom tap that became a mainstay on Broadway and in Hollywood

movies starting in the 1930s. Rogers and Astaire made ten Hollywood musicals, including *Top Hat* (1935), *Swing Time* (1936) and *Shall We Dance* (1937).

24   *'Cheek to Cheek'*: a song by Irving Berlin that Fred Astaire performed in the 1935 film *Top Hat*. 'Cheek to Cheek', which begins with the lines 'Heaven, I'm in heaven', describes a relationship where intimacy tops every other joy of life. 'Cheek to Cheek' was an extremely popular song and remains a well-known American standard.

25   *Oh as blond as the tassels on Golden Bantam corn*: Golden Bantam corn is a sweet yellow corn often grown in home gardens and eaten on the cob. As the plant matures, the corn ears sprout silky tassels that are nearly white and very finely textured. The blond hair typical of many Scandinavians was often compared to corn silks in both colour and texture.

26   *Charles won the All New England golf tournament, and Buzz came within a tenth of an inch of the gold medal in the pole vault – that was in the Tokyo Olympics*: the athletic achievements of Patricia's brothers are notable but both seem somehow secondary. New England, after all, is not that big a place, consisting of the states of Connecticut, Rhode Island, Massachusetts, Vermont, New Hampshire and Maine. Patricia's description of Buzz's Olympic performance – not silver medal-winning but 'within a tenth of an inch of the gold medal' – adds to the pathos of her description. The Summer Olympics took place in Tokyo in 1964, which indicates that Buzz was much older than Patricia.

30   *You've got to stop imitating your father*: while Leroy has suggested earlier that he and his father, a lawyer, have little in common, Patricia seems to disagree.

31   *just because your name was Sorgenson*: Sorgenson sounds like a typical Swedish name but it does not carry the same kind of prestigious historical weight as Hamilton. Leroy suggests that Patricia's family's pride comes from within, rather than being widely acknowledged by the community.

31   *The last human being I took on to help me tried to steal my half-inch Stanley chisel*: the Stanley company has made tools in Connecticut since 1843 and remains one of the best-known names in American handtools.

32   *And he's a Chapman – that's one of the oldest upstanding families in the county*: the Chapmans are one of the oldest families in New London County, Connecticut, the earliest settlers appearing as far back as 1657.

33   *two ounces of trust*: an ounce is approximately 28 grams. Since Leroy is speaking metaphorically here, two ounces means a trivial amount.

33   *They paid them fifty cents a week and called us dumb Swedes with strong backs and weak minds and did nothing but make us ridiculous*: Patricia's complaints reflect a historically accurate stereotype. Many Americans in the nineteenth century saw the new Swedish immigrants as fit only for manual labour and domestic service.

39   *Couldn't you do it on guitar?*: Patricia again prefers the smoother sounds of the European guitar to the twang of the African-derived banjo.

40   *All it is is a high hat and shorts*: Karen's costume includes the kind of top hat often worn by Fred Astaire and other tap dancers of the 1930s. Sometimes female dancers adopted the masculine top hat, either with a tuxedo or cutaway jacket, as part of their costume. Karen's variation, with satin dance shorts, a tailcoat and a walking stick, is particularly incongruous for a woman of her age, particularly as it is a vintage showgirl's outfit.

41   *shooting blanks*: Frick compares Karen's inability to function with a gun shooting empty cartridges. Blanks produce noise and smoke but no projectiles. Given her dislike of hunting, it seems a particularly insensitive comment.

41   *started from down below sea level myself, sixty acres of rocks and swampland is all we had*: Frick shows here that he shares Leroy's 'swamp Yankee' heritage, a fact that he has previously concealed. This revelation shows the authenticity of his appreciation of Patricia – he would have been unlikely to share this information with Leroy, with whom he was always competing.

43   *'Swanee River'*: the Stephen Foster song 'Old Folks at
     Home' is better known by its first line, 'Way down upon
     the Swanee River, far, far away'. Forster composed the
     music and lyrics in 1851 for the Christy Minstrels. While
     the Suwanee River is located in Florida, which adopted
     'Old Folks at Home' as the state song in 1935, Foster
     never saw the river, choosing the name solely for the
     sound and meter. From its inception, the song has
     enthralled listeners with its nostalgic images, and it has
     become one of the most popular folk songs of all time
     both inside and outside the United States. Throughout
     its history, the racial elements of the song, particularly
     the lyric's original exaggerated African-American
     dialect, have been interpreted in both positive and
     negative ways. Given Frick's earlier comments about
     'colored' and 'Negroes', one can assume that he would
     find the song embarrassing, even if his wife were not
     dancing to it. The lyric also mentions a banjo as part of
     the idyllic setting of the old home place. In the context
     of Karen's depression, the song's evocation of a happy
     past, now lost, is particularly poignant.

Questions for Further Study

1 How do the elements of comedy and tragedy interact throughout *The Last Yankee*?

2 In 'About Theatre Language', Miller says, 'The vision of the play [. . .] is intended to be both close-up and wide, psychological and social, subjective and objective.' How is this achieved or isn't it?

3 How might the play change if Dr Rockwell were a character on stage?

4 Who is the 'last Yankee'? What is the significance of the title?

5 Arthur Miller offers minimal instructions regarding the set. If you were designing the set for *The Last Yankee*, what elements would you pay attention to and why?

6 In his essay 'About Theatre Language', Miller wrote, 'Depression is far from being merely a question of an individual's illness.' How is this concept shown throughout the play?

7 In what ways are Frick and Karen the catalyst for Patricia's decision to leave at the end of the play?

8 How would the play change if the men were the patients and the women were the visitors?

9 Is *The Last Yankee* 'only' an American play? How might it work, if at all, in other national contexts?

10 In the second scene, Patricia tells Karen 'but everything's a fake, we all know that'. What does she mean by this statement? Use instances in the play to support your claim.

11 Analyse the way in which perceptions of class shape the views of the characters throughout the play.

12 What does the men's conversation in the first scene imply about their views of marriage? Compare their views to those the women reveal in the second scene.

13   This is a play that is often defined by its pauses. How do you imagine those pauses work on stage, and what might make that challenging for the actors?

14   Miller's characters repeatedly return to the subject of American businesses. What, in Miller's view, is the right role for business in America and how do you come to learn that? How might this idea be expanded beyond America's borders?

15   Discuss the themes of reality, disillusion and acceptance in the play.

16   How is Patricia and Leroy's marital relationship similar to Karen and Frick's? How is it different?

17   What kind of emotional resolution does *The Last Yankee* offer? Might differences in staging affect this final impression?

18   In this play of duets, can you identify a single protagonist and antagonist? How does the play change when you shift these roles from character to character?

19   If you were staging this play, would you have an actor play the unnamed Patient? Why or why not? What role does the sleeping figure play in *The Last Yankee*?

20   Characters in this play spend a considerable amount of time discussing Protestant religious observances and culture. What does this contribute to the play, and to your view of religion in America?

21   How might multi-racial casting affect the impact of this play in performance?

22   *The Last Yankee* features tap-dancing and banjo-playing. How might these symbolise escape or represent an alternative reality?

23   To what extent might it be said that the characters in this play are sleep-walking through their nation's history?

24   'The play's language has a surface of everyday realism, but its action is overtly stylized rather than "natural"' ('About Theatre Language'). Discuss how a director might choose to deal with this issue in a potential production.

25   If you were staging *The Last Yankee* as part of a double-bill, with what would you present it and why?

KATHERINE EGERTON is an assistant professor in the department of English, Theatre, and Communication at Berea College in Berea, Kentucky. Her published essays on Arthur Miller have appeared in the *Arthur Miller Journal, Text & Presentation 2008* and the *Journal of American Drama and Theatre*.

ENOCH BRATER is the Kenneth T. Rowe Collegiate Professor of Dramatic Literature at the University of Michigan. He has published widely in the field of modern drama, and is an internationally renowned expert on such figures as Samuel Beckett and Arthur Miller. His recent books include *Arthur Miller: A Playwright's Life and Works, Arthur Miller's America: Theater and Culture in a Time Of Change* and *Arthur Miller's Global Theater: How an American Playwright Is Performed on Stages around the World*.

Titles by Arthur Miller available from Methuen Drama

World Classics

MILLER PLAYS: 1
(All My Sons, Death of a Salesman, The Crucible,
A Memory of Two Mondays, A View from the Bridge)
ISBN 978 1 408 11130 7

MILLER PLAYS: 2
(The Misfits, After the Fall, Incident at Vichy, The Price, The
Creation of the World and Other Business, Playing for Time)
ISBN 978 1 408 11131 4

MILLER PLAYS: 3
(The American Clock, The Archbishop's Ceiling,
Two-Way Mirror)
ISBN 978 1 408 11132 1

MILLER PLAYS: 4
(The Golden Years, The Man Who Had All the Luck,
I Can't Remember Anything, Clara)
ISBN 978 1 408 11133 8

MILLER PLAYS: 5
(The Last Yankee, The Ride Down Mount Morgan,
Almost Everybody Wins)
ISBN 978 1 408 11134 5

MILLER PLAYS: 6
(Broken Glass, Mr Peters' Connections, Resurrection Blues,
Finishing the Picture)
ISBN 978 1 408 10685 3

Modern Plays

Broken Glass
ISBN 978 0 413 68190 4

The Man Who Had All the Luck
ISBN 978 1 408 10676 1

Scholarly Editions

Series Editor: Enoch Brater

After the Fall
edited by Brenda Murphy
ISBN 978 1 408 12312 6

All My Sons
edited by Toby Zinman
ISBN 978 1 408 10838 3

Broken Glass
edited by Alan Ackerman
ISBN 978 1 408 12884 8

The Crucible
edited by Susan C. W. Abbotson
ISBN 978 1 408 10839 0

The Last Yankee
edited by Katherine Egerton
ISBN 978 1 408 12315 7

The Price
edited by Jane K. Dominik
ISBN 978 1 408 12311 9

Death of a Salesman
edited by Enoch Brater
ISBN 978 1 408 108413

A Memory of Two Mondays
edited by Joshua Polster
ISBN 978 1 408 12316 4

A View from the Bridge
edited by Stephen Marino
ISBN 978 1 408 10840 6